Foul Deeds In Richmond and Kingston

TRUE CRIME FROM WHARNCLIFFE

Foul Deeds and Suspicious Deaths Series

Barking, Dagenham & Chadwell Heath
Barnsley
Bath
Bedford
Birmingham
Black Country
Blackburn and Hyndburn
Bolton
Bradford
Brighton
Bristol
Cambridge
Carlisle
Chesterfield
Colchester
Coventry
Croydon
Derby
Dublin
Durham
Ealing
Folkestone and Dover
Grimsby
Guernsey
Guildford
Halifax
Hampstead, Holborn and St Pancras
Huddersfield
Hull
Leeds
Leicester
Lewisham and Deptford
Liverpool
London's East End
London's West End
Manchester
Mansfield
More Foul Deeds Birmingham
More Foul Deeds Chesterfield
More Foul Deeds Wakefield
Newcastle
Newport
Norfolk
Northampton
Nottingham
Oxfordshire
Pontefract and Castleford
Portsmouth
Rotherham
Sheffield
Scunthorpe
Southend-on-Sea
Staffordshire and The Potteries
Stratford and South Warwickshire
Tees
Warwickshire
Wigan
York

OTHER TRUE CRIME BOOKS FROM WHARNCLIFFE

A–Z of Yorkshire Murder
Black Barnsley
Brighton Crime and Vice 1800–2000
Durham Executions
Essex Murders
Executions & Hangings in Newcastle and Morpeth
Norfolk Mayhem and Murder
Norwich Murders
Strangeways Hanged
The A–Z of London Murders
Unsolved Murders in Victorian and Edwardian London
Unsolved Norfolk Murders
Unsolved Yorkshire Murders
Yorkshire's Murderous Women

Foul Deeds In

RICHMOND & KINGSTON

JONATHAN OATES

First published in Great Britain in 2010 by
Wharncliffe Local History
an imprint of
Pen & Sword Books Ltd
47 Church Street
Barnsley
South Yorkshire
S70 2AS

ISBN 978 1 84563 125 3

A CIP catalogue record for this book is available from the British Library.

Typeset in 11/13pt Plantin by
Mac Style, Beverley, East Yorkshire

Printed and bound in the UK by
CPI Antony Rowe, Chippenham, Wiltshire

Pen & Sword Books Ltd incorporates the imprints of Pen & Sword Aviation, Pen & Sword Maritime, Pen & Sword Military, Wharncliffe Local History, Pen and Sword Select, Pen and Sword Military Classics and
Leo Cooper.

For a complete list of Pen & Sword titles please contact
PEN & SWORD BOOKS LIMITED
47 Church Street, Barnsley, South Yorkshire, S70 2AS, England
E-mail: enquiries@pen-and-sword.co.uk
Website: www.pen-and-sword.co.uk

Contents

Acknowledgements

The author wishes to thank those staff at Richmond Local Studies Centre, Kingston Local Studies Centre, Hammersmith and Fulham Local Studies Centre, the London Metropolitan Archives, the Surrey History Centre and The National Archives, for assisting in his enquiries. These included fetching maps, assisting with microfilm and archives, and dealing with Freedom of Information enquiries. Without them and their historical material, this book could not have been written. Staff at the Broadmoor Hospital dealt efficiently with enquiries. John Coulter, was, as always, helpful with his knowledge, too.

This book is dedicated to John.

Introduction

When Richmond's history is mentioned, most people think of Hampton Court and Henry VIII. Crime does not obviously spring to mind, whereas it would if Whitechapel or Notting Hill were mentioned. Some books about Richmond and Kingston do not even allude to it. Yet criminal activity does not recognise geographical or social boundaries and this book aims to demonstrate this. *Foul Deeds in Richmond and Kingston* covers a number of serious crimes which took place in what are now the London Boroughs of Kingston on Thames (Norbiton, Surbiton and Kingston itself) and Richmond (Barnes, Mortlake, Teddington, Hampton, Twickenham and Richmond), from the early nineteenth century until the 1950s. Some are shocking indeed, such as the murder and dissection of Mrs Thomas, by her servant, Kate Webster, in Richmond, in 1879 and the savage killing of two teenagers on the Teddington towpath in the 1950s. The alleged poisoning of Louisa Bankes in 1859 was once a *cause celebre*, but all these have now been mostly forgotten, except by crime buffs. In their day all were reported as national news. There are also unsolved murders, killings in Richmond Park and other foul crimes.

This book does not aim to be comprehensive, due to limitations of space; therefore other murders in these districts can be found listed in the appendix. Rather I have chosen ones for which there is an appreciable amount of information. Those which occurred elsewhere, but have local connections, are also omitted – Buster Edwards of Great Train Robbery infamy resided at St Margaret's Road, Twickenham, and hid some of the loot at a friend's in Kingston, for instance.

Many people believe that the internet is the fount of all knowledge, but only three of the cases in this book feature there (those referred to in the first paragraph), and not in any great detail. It is the paper-based sources which are of most use. Chiefly, the evidence used here has been taken from the police files found at The National Archives, Kew. These include reports made by the chief inspector who was in charge of the investigation, reports by doctors, witnesses, other police officers and those accused of the crime. Some of these sources have only recently been made available to the public. They vary enormously in scope – those for the nineteenth century murders are quite thin, compared to the later ones, for example.

Other key sources include the press. These are the local newspapers, such as the *Surrey Comet*. These have detailed reports of the discovery of the crime, inquests and trials. The national newspapers are also useful, especially *The Times* online digital database, which although not as detailed for the twentieth century, does enable a researcher to find cases which otherwise would be difficult to locate. Of course, there is much overlap between the press and the police files, but there is also different information found in both, too.

I have also used sources well known to the experienced geneaologist in order to flesh out the principal characters in the text: census returns, wills, parish registers, military records and so forth.

The book begins with an introductory chapter about the districts in which the crimes were committed, and a survey of policing and law and order in these places. Then the cases will be discussed in chronological order, from 1812–1953.

My qualifications for writing this book are that I have been a published historian for a decade. A qualified and experienced London archivist, my knowledge of the relevant sources is not inconsiderable. And I have had seven books about crime history published already. Finally, I resided in Richmond in 1992, working at the Surrey Record Office when it was located at Kingston.

CHAPTER 1

Richmond and Kingston: A Brief History

Nothing in the neighbourhood is better known or more delightful than the view from Richmond Hill and Terrace.

It is, of course, impossible to give a detailed account of the history of these districts in about 2,000 words. The interested reader can consult numerous books on this topic if he or she wishes. This chapter is merely a brief overview of the locations where the crimes covered thereafter occurred.

For many centuries, places such as Richmond, Kingston, Teddington and Twickenham were villages along the river Thames, seemingly far to the west of London (Richmond is 15½ miles from London; Kingston 20). In fact, this was the case until the late nineteenth century. Twickenham and Kingston date from Saxon times; indeed the latter was not a inconsiderable town then. Saxon Kings were crowned there in the tenth century (the Coronation Stone is on display in the town to this day) and as late as the sixteenth century, the nearest bridge over the Thames to the west of London Bridge was at Kingston.

Royal connections persisted into the Middle Ages and beyond. There was a royal palace at Richmond which was used by Edward III and his grandson, Richard II. It was rebuilt in the fifteenth century. In fact, at this time, Richmond was known as Sheen, and only had a name change at the end of the fifteenth century. This was when Henry, Duke of Richmond, and the first Tudor monarch (Henry VII), had one of his palaces here and had the parish renamed. This palace was demolished on Cromwell's orders in 1648. But there was a better known one. This was Hampton Court, one of Henry VIII's chief palaces. His daughter, Elizabeth I, died at

Old Palace Gates, Richmond. Author's collection

Richmond in 1603 and a number of her successors in the seventeenth and eighteenth centuries were well acquainted with Richmond and Hampton Court. From 1837, the latter was thrown open to the public and continues to delight the tourists. Kingston was the scene of strife in the Middle Ages with its castle being destroyed in 1264 and skirmishes occurred there in the Civil War of the 1640s, when a Duke's brother was killed.

St Mary's church, Richmond. Author's collection

In the eighteenth and nineteenth centuries, a number of celebrities resided in these districts, in large houses near to the river, where access to London was easy, yet their homes were in a delightful setting. These figures included, at Twickenham, famous writers such as Alexander Pope and Horace Walpole. Later, famous inhabitants were Dickens and Tennyson and the numerous pretenders to the French throne who lived here in the following century. At the beginning of the twentieth century the deposed King Manoel of Portugal resided here. The founder of *The Times*, John Walter, lived in Teddington, as did the famous comic actress Peggy Woffington. Most of these large mansions were demolished in the early twentieth century.

Districts west of London on the Thames, apart from Brentford, did not develop the industrial character associated with those in central or east London, such as Limehouse, Wapping and Woolwich. This is because the great trading ports were naturally on that part of the Thames which was nearest its estuary; likewise for Royal Navy establishments. When industry did arrive to the west of the capital, in the early twentieth century, it was situated near major rail and road links: at Acton, Southall, Greenford, Brentford and Hounslow. An exception is at Teddington, where there was a large candle factory in the nineteenth century. Another industrial site was the National Physical Laboratory at Teddington, 'that now gigantic complex of workshops', founded in about 1900, one of whose employees was, briefly in the 1920s, one Sydney Goulter (see Chapter 13). Thus these districts remained chiefly residential. Small-scale commercial enterprises were located in Twickenham, such as fruit gardening, lamphrey fishing and there was also a linseed mill.

The nineteenth and twentieth centuries saw rapid change, as they did all around the capital, transforming once rural retreats to teeming suburbs. In part the blame can be laid at the feet of the transport revolution, which was a cause of great change throughout Britain; and in part it was due to the population explosion and the fact that many more people were becoming richer than they ever had before. Richmond had a railway station from 1846 which was rebuilt in 1937.

By 1881, there were numerous rail links from Richmond to London. The London and South Western railway meant that London Waterloo was only 9¾ miles away and the commuting time was a little under half an hour. Trains also ran to Aldgate and Broad Street, taking an hour, and were clearly a boon for City workers. Mansion House and Ludgate Hill were other central London destinations available from Richmond station. An annual first-class season ticket from Richmond to Waterloo and back cost £16 in 1886; second class was £12. For Kingston, Norbiton and Surbiton, these charges were £18 and £13 10s respectively; though the journey time was twenty-five minutes, the distance was twelve miles. These were still, however high enough to prohibit the average working man from using trains as his regular transport to work. If the commuter did not want to walk home from the railway station, he could catch one of the numerous 'flies' (horse-drawn cabs), which met the incoming train.

It was in the early twentieth century, with the introduction of trams, that the less affluent could afford the pleasures of commuting to work each day. Electric trams began to run from Twickenham from 1903.

A contemporary publication (1887) noted, as far as Richmond is concerned:

> From a small village Richmond has rapidly grown into a considerable town, and building is still actively carried on. Its convenient distance from London, beautiful and healthy situation, and pleasant neighbourhood, all combine to make it attractive to those who have daily business in town, and still want a certain amount of fresh air, while the railway facilities have been greatly increased and improved of late years. Houses, therefore, of all classes, from the mansion to the cottage, have lately sprung up in all directions.

Such suburbanisation continued apace in the twentieth century, too. One commentator, writing in the 1930s, noted:

> Less than twenty years ago the approach from London, by tramcar, through Isleworth, provided an enchanted panorama

Star and Garter Home, Richmond. Author's collection

of orchards ... Now it [Twickenham] is becoming the complete suburb: rows and rows of 'Houses of Artistry' – all just alike – forests of crazy wireless masts, acres of screaming hoardings, petrol pumps, and cinema posters, streets vulgar at worst and undistinguished at best.

The Thames near Richmond. Author's collection

As to Teddington, it was 'a built up area with no special attractions'.

Population certainly soared. In 1801, there were 699 inhabitants in Teddington; in 1911, there were 17,847. In Twickenham the increase was from 3,138 to 29,367 over the same period. In the next half century, the population had doubled again. Richmond and Kingston had become towns in the late Victorian era, having populations of 22,000 and 17,000 respectively by 1881; though by 1901 these figures were 31,672 and 34,375.

Yet Richmond was still undoubtedly an attractive place, despite its transformation from the home of royalty and other celebrities. In the 1890s, Richmond was described in *The Times* as being the Queen of the Suburbs, (and Surbiton was Queen of the London Suburbs) a decade before Ealing adopted that soubriquet. In part this was because of the large number of open spaces. The principal one of these is Richmond Park, consisting of 2,250 acres and being adjacent to Wimbledon Common. It was described as being 'some eight miles in circumference, and affording an infinite variety of delightful walks and drives'. One could say the same about other open spaces in the vicinity. Marble Hill Park in Twickenham, purchased by the London County Council in 1904 was another important acquisition, although only seventy-two acres, it also possessed fine views of the river. Hampton Court and its environs are another important beauty spot, too. The retention of these open spaces was important in retaining the pleasant character of these districts. Yet to remind us that evil had not been banished from them, we need to recall that there were two murders in Richmond Park between the world wars (told in Chapters 13 and 14).

The river which runs by all these districts was another attraction. Boat races along the Thames were popular from the Victorian era onwards. Boating clubs flourished. There was a Kingston Rowing Club and an annual Kingston Rowing Regatta. Steam ferries along the Thames to and from London were another attraction. Anglers could buy cheap tickets at the weekends. Locks were erected on this part of the Thames. A large lock was constructed at Teddington in 1905, marking the furthermost boundary of the authority of the Port of London, seventeen miles from Westminster Bridge and where the Thames ceases to be tidal. This is also the largest in the Thames, measuring 650 feet in length and 25 feet in width. It was the scene of two brutal murders in 1953 (recounted in Chapter 20).

Visitors certainly saw Richmond and the other Thameside districts as attractive places to spend their leisure time. In 1886, it was noted that it was 'one of the most favourite excursions of Londoners of all classes'. The views of the river were magnificent:

> Nothing in the neighbourhood is better known or more delightful than the view from Richmond Hill and Terrace, and when Sir Walter Scott described it as an unrivalled landscape, he was hardly saying too much.

Hotels and boarding houses catered for the tourist. In 1886, *Richmond Hill Hotel* charged between 10s 6d to £2 2s for a room per week. More hotels appeared in the following decade. There were three hotels in late Victorian Kingston, all located in the Market Place.

Apart from the Thames, Richmond and Twickenham are also well known for their sporting attractions. Dr Watson is noted as playing rugby at Richmond, and Twickenham, 'for our governing classes to whom it primarily suggests Rugby Football, college ties and a comfortable feeling of athletic exclusiveness'.

These towns also witnessed the growth of civil amenities and the arrival of more and diverse places of religion to cater for a more numerous population. Late Victorian Richmond boasted a theatre, a library, a fire station, a police station, a hospital, almshouses, four Anglican churches, a Catholic church and six nonconformist chapels. The parish church of St Mary Magdalen was 'of the hideous red brick usual hereabouts', though it did contain a number of interesting memorials to former residents of note, but the other churches were 'modern erections of no special attractiveness'. Post from London arrived five times daily in 1887 and there were nine daily collections to town at this time.

Administratively, the government of these growing settlements changed as time went by. Until the nineteenth century, each parish governed itself, with loose supervision by the magistrates at Middlesex and Surrey Quarter Sessions, depending on whether the parish was to the north/west of the Thames or not. Care of the poor and upkeep of local roads and the parish church were the principal concern of parish government. However, as the responsibilities of local government increased, change was thought necessary. Ecclesiastical and civil government split in the nineteenth century. Local authorities became responsible for medical provision, sanitation and education. Voluntarily funded hospitals were built. Parishes were amalgamated with each other. In 1937, the borough of Twickenham incorporated Teddington, and in 1965 it was added to the borough of Richmond; likewise, Surbiton and Norbiton were joined to Kingston in this year to form another London borough.

These districts include some of London's most attractive and exclusive ones to this day as they did in the time of Henry VIII or Horace Walpole, though the social mix has became far more diverse as these Thameside villages became towns in the late nineteenth centuries and then suburbs in the twentieth. Yet though a long distance from the East End, they were also the back cloth to a number of hideously shocking crimes and it is with these that the rest of the book deals.

In the period covered by this book, these districts were policed by the Metropolitan Police. This force had been founded in 1829 by Sir Robert Peel. Initially it had only covered central London. In 1839 it had been extended to cover the whole of Middlesex and parts of Surrey, Essex and Kent. This area was divided into divisions, each under a Chief Superintendent, and each division had a number of stations, each headed by an Inspector.

Twickenham, Hampton and Teddington, being north of the Thames, were in the county of Middlesex, and were in division T, as were other parts of western Middlesex, including Ealing and Acton. Twickenham Police Station was on London Road and that at Teddington was on Church Road. Incidentally, the Metropolitan and City of London Police Orphanage was at

Wellesley Road, Hampton Road. It was founded in 1870 and extended in 1879. It catered for 250 boys and girls. The Police War Memorial Hospital was founded nearby in 1923 and opened by the Prince of Wales (briefly Edward VIII).

Richmond and Kingston, being in Surrey, were part of division V.

A police station was erected at Richmond in 1840, on Princes Street, and there it remained for the next fifty years. In 1890, a new one was built in George Street, ironically near to the site of the old watch house. Finally, in 1912, the station relocated to Red Lion Street, where it currently (2010) still stands. It was to this station that Sydney Goulter was conveyed in 1927 (see Chapter 13)

Once a murder had occurred, and a corpse discovered, there were two principal events which had to take place. Firstly, an inquest was held to determine who had died, and how and who was responsible. A coroner would oversee such proceedings and a jury had to decide the verdict. Then there was the magistrates' court which would hear evidence, examine clues and witnesses and, if possible, pronounce who was responsible. If someone was named, they could be arrested and gaoled (often in Wandsworth prison), pending

Kingston multi-view card. Author's collection

trial either at the Old Bailey or the Surrey Assizes, both courts being able to deal with murder. Should guilt be found, then a death sentence could be pronounced or the guilty could face either prison or Broadmoor, depending on whether they were judged to be mentally responsible for their actions.

Police methods in the period covered by this book were primitive by modern standards, but forensic science was being developed in the first half of the twentieth century. One key figure to appear in murder cases was Sir Bernard Spilsbury (1877-1947), a Home Office pathologist who features in a number of cases here. He became a household name in 1910 when he took part in the Crippen case, but it is now thought that he was far from infallible.

Having briefly set the scene, we shall now learn about nineteen cases of murder, suicide and suspicious death in Richmond and Kingston, not all of which were solved.

CHAPTER 2

Death of the Aristocrats 1812

Few now, perhaps, of the teeming multitude, who pass to and fro daily know of this tragic scene.

The tragic scene referred to above by a writer in 1903 refers to an address in Barnes Terrace, and those passing by unknowingly would have included the present author, when he was investigating the Elizabeth Figg murder of 1959 – her body was found in Duke's Meadow, on the opposite side of the river to where an earlier tragedy occurred.

The first French Revolution, which began in 1789, became bloodier as the years progressed, culminating in the Reign of

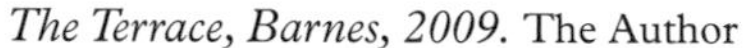

The Terrace, Barnes, 2009. The Author

Terror, in 1793–94. Many Frenchmen fled to Britain to escape death. This was not just those who opposed the revolution outright, but also those who favoured reforms, but had fallen out with France's new masters. Many settled in Twickenham, Richmond and Barnes, including Louis Philippe (1773–1850), who later became King of France in 1830–48. These Thameside districts were indeed delightful tranquil villages in themselves, but were also close to the capital and so to places of entertainment and power.

One such nobleman was the Comte D'Antraigues, or to give him his full name, Emmanuel Louis Henri Alexandre de Launay. He was distantly related to the French royal family, the Bourbons, and was born in 1753. Aged fourteen, he joined the Royal Guards as an officer, but did not see much military service as he left under a cloud of allegations of cowardice. After a spell of foreign travel, he returned to France hostile to both religion and the established monarchical order, and entered politics. He married Madame St Huberti, an actress at the Theatre Francoise who had become very wealthy by her professional talents. She was also an accomplished singer and often performed at fashionable parties. She was four years younger than her husband. In 1812, their son, Jules, was studying law in Manchester.

Although elected to the States General in 1789, the Comte began to oppose the revolutionary changes then sweeping France. He became involved in espionage, in the 1790s, in the employ of the Spanish court and then on behalf of the Germans and Russians, but when they had been temporarily knocked out of the fight against Napoleon, from about 1807, for the British. Apparently he had been present at the negotiations between Napoleon and Tsar Alexander at the Treaty of Tilsit in that year. He had then passed on what he knew to George Canning of the Foreign Office (later Foreign Secretary and then Prime Minister). His services were seen as valuable because he was in receipt of government money.

From about 1807 or 1808 they were living in a house on the upper part of Barnes Terrace, 'a line of good houses', half a mile from the parish church and near to the Thames. This was not in the style to which the Comte had been born, but it was still far above average. They kept a coach, a coachman (William Henditch), footman and a servant out of livery. The latter was also termed a valet. In July 1812, this post was held by an Italian, named Lawrence Stelli, who had been with them for three months. The family also had a town house in Queen Anne Street, in London's West End.

One morning, Wednesday 22 July 1812, the coach had been ordered for 8 o'clock, for the Comte and Comtesse desired to go to London. It arrived at just before 9, and the two were ready to depart, the Comte descending the stairs and his wife was just crossing the threshold of their house. It was then that the report of a pistol was heard in the passage. This seems to have had no effect. Then the firer, who was none other than Stelli, threw his gun away, and rushed up the stairs, passing his master as he did so. He immediately returned, knife in hand, and plunged it up to the hilt in the Comte's shoulder. Ironically, the Comte had bought this knife decades earlier, in Constantinople, and kept it in his bedroom for self defence.

Quickly pulling his deadly weapon out of his victim, he continued through the house. Finding his mistress on the door step, he attacked her, stabbing her in the left breast. No sooner than he had done so, than the injured Comte appeared before him and evidently stood just outside the house. Stelli ran back into the house and up the stairs, chased by the bleeding man, who was now weak and faint. No one dare follow them. Soon after both were upstairs, a shot rang out and then all was quiet.

The servants eventually plucked up the courage to investigate. They found their mistress dying on the front door. More resolution was needed for them to venture up the staircase, but they finally did so. To their horror, the Comte was lying across his own bed, groaning heavily and evidently dying. By his side was his murderer, who was dead. Apparently he had placed the barrel of a pistol in his mouth and pulled the trigger. The Comte died about twenty-five minutes after he had been stabbed and did not utter another word. His wife died five minutes before he did, and again, she never spoke again.

The mystery was how this appalling double murder had happened, and why. The pistols and knife used in the crimes were usually hanging in the Comte's bedroom, and the pistols were always loaded. A month before the murder, the Comtesse and her female servants heard a pistol being fired in her husband's room. Upon investigation, once the cloud of smoke had dissipated, they saw Stelli there. For some reason, he had fired into the wainscoat, and did not deny he had fired his master's pistols.

Ten minutes before he attacked his master on that fatal day, he had had a glass of gin in *The White Hart*, the pub opposite his place of work, but he was not drunk. Nor was he motivated by politics and he had not quarrelled with his master. His motive was that he had heard his master and mistress discussing the termination of his employment, with the aim of discharging him in a few days. This may have been because of his eccentric behaviour, as outlined in the paragraph above. The inquest was held at *The White Hart* on the following day.

Stelli was clearly a man who was unsound in mind, and when his employers realised this, they naturally wanted to discharge him for the sake of their peace of mind. Yet their servant reacted violently to their plan and taking them both by

The White Hart, *Barnes, 2009.* The Author

Barnes church. Author's collection

surprise, used the Comte's own weapons on him and his wife, and so a treble tragedy ensued in Barnes.

Local tradition states that Stelli's body was buried at the crossroads on Barnes Common, because of the belief that the ghost of this suicide would be unable to roam since it was confused by the four ways leading from its burial place.

CHAPTER 3

Did Dr Smethurst Murder his Wife? 1859

When a doctor goes wrong he is the first of criminals. He has the nerve and he has the knowledge.

So spoke Sherlock Holmes in *The Adventure of the Speckled Band*, one of the most famous stories by Conan Doyle. The Victorian doctor is often seen, at least in fiction, as a sinister figure, able to consign his prey to asylums, to poison his victims or being able to dissect them – the erroneous stereotype of Jack the Ripper being a doctor still exists in the popular mind. But some doctors did poison their victims in reality. Doctors William Palmer (1824–56) and Edward Pritchard (1825–65) are among the most famous examples of their kind. But mystery surrounds Dr Thomas Smethurst's actions.

It is presumed that on 10 March 1828, the bells of St Mark's, Kennington, rang out. This would have been to celebrate the marriage of Thomas Smethurst and Mary Durham. Mr William Otter was the officiating clergyman and the marriage was by special licence from the bishop, not by banns, as usual. The groom was born in Great Budworth, Cheshire, on 2 January 1805, while his bride was a mature woman of forty-two (being born in Hornsey, Middlesex, in about 1786). Smethurst had lived some of his early years in Lancashire, the family moving to Preston when he was very young, and he had at least two brothers, James and William. In 1858, he noted that his father was called William and was a gentleman; this is certainly possible for the younger William was described as being of 'independent means' in 1851. His bride had previously gone under the name of Johnson, living with a man of the same surname. It seems she may have been a servant and may have been legally married to Johnson or

St Mark's church, Kennington. Author's collection

Laporte as he also called himself. She may have married Smethurst due to his future prospects, but he was briefly in trouble with the law in 1828, for obtaining goods under false pretences, though was never sentenced.

Little is known of the married life of the Smethursts, but it seemed to go well, although there were no children. His wife stated in 1859, 'We have lived together in perfect happiness and contentment' and he had nursed her back to health when ill. Her husband made similar remarks, 'we have lived together happily a good number of years.'

Smethurst began a medical career, having undergone an apprenticeship under the Society of Apothecaries from 15 November 1824 and had been with James Hay of Newgate Street for five years. He had attended courses in anatomy and physiology at the Westminster Dispensary. He was examined on 28 March 1833, but failed, so took his examination in the following year, twice, before successfully qualifying on 18 September 1834. However, on 25 March of that year, he had already begun operating as a surgeon, chemist and druggist in Clapham Street, Stockwell, insuring the premises for £500, and this was where he lived, and remained there until at least 1838. In 1841, he lived in Preston by Wingham, Kent. In the following year he spent 'a residence of some months' at Grafenberg, in Bavaria. There he observed the hydrotherapeutic establishments and on his return to England, he had a book, *Hydrotherepia: Or the Water Cure, Being a Practical View of the Cure in all its Bearings, Exhibiting the Great Utility of Water as a Preservative of Health and Remedy for Disease*, published in 1843 and which was republished in the early twenty-first century. He said it was based on 'careful study, diligent inquiries and observations' and claimed that 'in water we have one of the most powerful therapeutic agents yet discovered'.

It was also at this time that the initials 'M.D.' were first seen after his name, though they are not listed in his entry in *The Medical Directory*. It is certain that he bought his degree in medicine, which was then quite easy to do. He had two medical practitioners, who had known him for some time sign a certificate that he was competent, then sent a fee to a legitimate university, who would send him his degree. Such initials after his name would increase his repute and standing and thus encourage greater custom. According to the 1851 census he had his degree from St Andrew's University, Scotland, but other sources mention Erlangen and Giessen, both in Bavaria and not far from Grafenberg and it is probable he bought his degree from one of these two.

By 1843 the Smethursts lived at Spencer House, Ramsgate, and had founded one of only four hydrotherapic establishments in England. But they did not stay there too long, for in 1847 they were at Harrington Square, north London. Moving on again, in 1851 they were at Moor End Park, Farnham, Surrey. From about 1850–55, he ran a hydropathic establishment there. He seems to have been at least moderately successful, for in 1859 a patient fondly recalled his treating him. Furthermore, they had three domestic servants listed as living with them. In 1855, Smethurst sold his practice to Edward Wickstead Lane. This was the last time he practised medicine. The couple then toured around the Continent, 'travelling about and living in Paris and also at different places in Germany'. Smethurst was reasonably well off, and, according to his brother James, had an income of about £240 per annum from property, plus fees from occasional private commissions.

In 1859, Smethurst was described as 'rather stout, swarthy complexion, with dark moustaches'.

However, from about June 1858, the Smethursts were living at Joseph Smith's boarding house at 4 Rifle Terrace, Bayswater (now the south-east part of Queensway). Mrs Smethurst was now aged seventy-two and her husband fifty-three. By the autumn, another occupant was a younger woman, Isabella Bankes (aged forty-two), a woman of independent means (about £480 pa), who will play an important part in the unfolding drama. Little is known about her, except that her (probably late) father, George Bankes, was styled a gentleman in a description in 1858 and she had an unmarried sister, Louisa, who lived in London and was also of independent means, both daughters living off the interest from investments. She began living at the same house as the Smethursts on 20 September 1858. Isabella was not apparently in the best of health, suffering from sickness, nausea and had had to leave the dinner table on two occasions.

They all seem to co-habit on the best of terms. Smith later recalled:

> Miss Bankes was in the habit of associating with Dr and Mrs Smethurst – the lady sat at the same table, and took the same meals, and was always recognised as Dr Smethurst's wife – Miss Bankes was quite on intimate terms with Mrs Smethurst – during the time they were living together I have seen Miss Bankes' sister call on her, on more than one occasion – I have seen Miss Bankes, her sister Miss Louisa Bankes, and Mrs Smethurst, taking their meals or luncheon together – as long as I knew Dr Smethurst his conduct was quite that of a gentleman; it was that of an amiable, well-behaved, kind person … he was very attentive towards his wife.

These amicable relations were only a veneer. Mrs Smith, the landlord's wife, gave Miss Bankes orders to quit on 29 November, because of 'improper familiarity' between her and the Smethursts. Mrs Smethurst later recalled that it was Miss Bankes who had encouraged her husband to stray. She did not go far. She went to a lodging house in Kildare Road, Bayswater, and went out for a walk every day, to go to Clifton for the good of her health. Yet events were to take a decisive turn for the dramatic on 9 December at the parish church of Battersea. It was there and then that Smethurst and Miss Bankes married, thus the former committed bigamy. James Spice, the parish clerk, witnessed the event. Smethurst left the boarding house on 12 December. However, Mrs Smethurst stayed on until at least June 1859. He visited her on several occasions thereafter, paying her weekly rent of £1 5s and frequently wrote to her.

Smethurst later claimed:

> I declare that my wife was aware of the attachment that existed between me and Miss Bankes, and that it was arranged that she should never trouble me or make any enquiries after me, and I was to visit her when I pleased, and nothing was to be said in my absence.

Old Palace Terrace, 2009. The Author

Smethurst also later claimed that he and Miss Bankes were passionately in love, and that only marriage would do, in order to maintain the respectability of his love and prevent her from any self reproach. He said that they were only waiting for the death of his first wife, now in her early seventies, which he did not think would be long. Although divorce was slightly easier after the Divorce Act of 1858, it was an expensive and time consuming activity, as well as a very public one, so was not to be undertaken lightly. Few did so.

It is not known where the 'newly weds' were for the next two months, but on 4 February, they had taken rooms in 6 Old Palace Terrace, Richmond Green, Richmond, paying 18s per week. Mrs Anne Robinson, the landlady, said that Isabella was in good health on arrival. But by late March she was suffering from sickness and diarrhoea. Smethurst proclaimed that it was a bilious attack. He supplied his 'wife' with all her meals. Yet he was unhappy with his diagnosis, for he summoned one Dr Julius, a local physician, as recommended by Mrs Robinson, but nonetheless, the vomiting and sickness carried on until 15 April, when the two left, apparently because Smethurst said he could not afford the new weekly rent which had risen by five shillings.

During their stay, Smethurst often went up to London. Isabella often complained of having no appetite, but when the landlady's daughter gave her an egg, she ate it and enjoyed it. When she returned from walks, she was exhausted. Yet there was every sign of Smethurst behaving affectionately towards her and her illness occurred when he was absent as well as when he was with her.

On 15 April, the pair were living at 10 Alma Villas (now part of Rosemont Road), renting a sitting room and a bedroom. They travelled there in a cab, and Mrs Susannah Wheatley, the proprietor, recalled that Isabella was scarcely able to walk, and had to go to her bed as soon as she arrived. Refusing the services of a doctor, allegedly on the grounds of cost, Smethurst declared that no one could tend her but himself and he had sole access to her and brought up all her meals to her room. She was only once seen in the sitting room. Mrs Wheatley offered to act a nurse, but Smethurst declined,

Alma Villas, Rosemont Road, 2009. The Author

though he did allow her to make his 'wife' some tapioca pudding; on the first occasion this was liked, on the second, it was thought to be bitter and not drunk. Again, the couple seemed very happy together.

Smethurst wrote to Louisa Bankes on 20 April, requesting that she visit. She did so and found her sister to be in an excitable state, but was unable to see her sister alone for more than a minute. Louisa suggested that a doctor known to their family, one Lane, be called in, but her sister refused, as did her ever present husband. Louisa offered to make some dessert for her sister, but Smethurst refused to allow this. He also mentioned that his wife's latest dividend under her late father's will was not as much as it normally was. On her departure, Isabella told Louisa that she wanted to see her again, and soon.

There were a few letters by Smethurst to Louisa, asking her not to visit because the excitement would upset Isabella. Yet on 30 April he wrote again. Isabella's condition had deteriorated. She may have believed she was on her deathbed, because that morning she called Mr Senior, a Richmond solicitor, and made her will. This left everything, except a brooch, to

Smethurst 'her sincere and beloved friend'. This was about £1,740, but the interest she was paid on a further £5,000 ended with her death. Louisa went to Richmond again, and saw her sister, who was by now unable to speak. As before, Smethurst stayed with the two sisters. She brought some soup for Isabella and allowed Smethurst to stir it. On eating it, she was at once sick. Smethurst explained that Isabella was in great pain, despite the pills provided by one Dr Todd, which had caused burning sensations all over her body.

Jemima Chetwood, a nurse, was hired on 2 May at the advice of Dr Julius' assistant, and she and Louisa attended Isabella, giving her arrow root and similar. Never once did she vomit again. She also drank tea without any problems. Yet at 11 am on 3 May, Isabella died in great agony. Smethurst refused to give any money for the nurse's services, because he said he had been opposed to the idea.

By this time, Smethurst was suspected by Dr Julius of poisoning her and was briefly taken into custody by Inspector McIntyre, of the local police, but was allowed to return to Isabella before she died.

On the day after Isabella's death, Smethurst was brought before the Richmond magistrates. He was accused of having caused Isabella's death by arsenic poisoning in order to financially benefit by her death. Dr Julius suspected Smethurst of poisoning her on the grounds that the medicine he had been supplying to her was not working and therefore something untoward must be happening. Samples from the deceased were sent to Dr Taylor of Guy's Hospital to analyse and he found traces of arsenic therein, but only in small quantities and insufficient to cause death. A post mortem found the liver and stomach to be inflamed, which was a symptom of, amongst other ailments, arsenic poisoning. Smethurst was then remanded in custody for a further hearing once more evidence had been amassed.

The next hearing took place at Richmond on 20 May. The investigation had subsequently involved the examination of the large number of medicine bottles that had been found in Smethurst and Isabella's rooms. One was found to contain chloride of potash which could cause inflammation. Quinine mixture in another bottle could produce arsenic if mixed with other substances. Yet a minute examination of the deceased's stomach and organs failed to discover any arsenic.

Other doctors gave their views. One, Dr Bird, who had seen Isabella in Richmond whilst alive, did not think she had suffered from dysentery and was at a loss to account for her symptoms. Arsenic or antimony, another poison, might result in them. Arsenic was easily obtainable and was a very commonly used poison.

Frederick Caudle, Dr Julius' assistant had prepared the medicines for his employer. He stated that neither arsenic nor antimony had been supplied in any of the preparations he had made up. Dr Todd attested to her suffering from vomiting and diarrhoea.

Dr Taylor summed up what he and most of the other doctors were thinking, when he said, 'I have no doubt that the cause of death is inflammation, caused by irritating poisons. Taking all the matters into consideration, I can only account for death by supposing that it had been the result of antimony and arsenic administered in small doses, and at intervals'. With that, and the support of a colleague from the same hospital, Dr Odling, Smethurst was formally committed for trial at the Old Bailey.

The trial was set for July, but had to be postponed until the following month because of the illness of a juror. When it actually began on 15 August, Smethurst pleaded 'not guilty' to the charge of murder. The prosecution began with a history of the prisoner's relations with Isabella Bankes, of her illness and then death. Much of the evidence was given by doctors Bird, Julius and the others mentioned, most of whom had no experience of dealing with cases of arsenic poisoning, it should be noted. Some were knowledgeable about dysentery overseas and amongst men. One key statement was by Dr Taylor, who stated that the copper strip on which he had tested for arsenic had been contaminated, thus rendering his evidence invalid. Another piece of crucial evidence was that Isabella was about six weeks pregnant on death. Vomiting and diarrhoea often occur in the early stages of pregnancy. Attention was also drawn to Smethurst's financial position. He had ceased to practice as a surgeon for some years and is not known to have any significant source of income. In April 1859, he only had between £100-150 in his account at the London and Westminster Bank. Later that month, £71 5s was added to this, from Isabella's income.

A number of doctors were called for the defence. They stated that Isabella might have died due to complications in the pregnancy or by dysentery. The lack of evidence about arsenic was also pointed out. It was also noted that Smethurst stood to lose financially by Isabella's death, because, although gaining a lump sum of £1,700, he would be losing a regular monthly income of just over £71. Furthermore, the £1,700 was not in ready money but was tied up in a mortgage. Smethurst's actions were also commented upon. He had called in doctors to help his wife, he had allowed others access to her and had tended to her himself. These were hardly the actions of a guilty man. It is also worth noting that no one could produce an entry in a poison book with Smethurst's signature on it, though perhaps this was an omission of the police and prosecution. Anyone buying arsenic would have had to have made such a declaration, but no one showed Smethurst to have had done so, indicating that he probably had not.

It had been a trial which had lasted five days, finishing on Friday 19 August. It was a complex and technical case. Sir Jonathan Pollock, the Chief Baron and judge, summed up against the prisoner. The jury retired for forty minutes. On their return, they informed the court that they had found Smethurst to be guilty. The death sentence was duly passed, and then Smethurst spoke for twenty-five minutes, an unusually long time. As ever, he was calm and emotionless, telling everyone about his innocence.

After the verdict had been given, the condemned man was sent to Horsemonger Gaol. A date for his execution was set, 31 August, and he began having discussions with the prison chaplain. Many people wished to see him, and he continued to protest his innocence to all he spoke to. Cynics recalled that Dr Palmer had done likewise. Yet in Smethurst's case, there seemed valid reasons for doubting his guilt. Many scientists and medical men wrote to the newspapers to support him (even Mary Smethurst wrote to protest at her erring husband's fate), though the jury who had decided his fate stuck to their decision.

Little did the jury know it, but the most famous writer of the day, Charles Dickens (1812–70) agreed with them. Known to his readers both then and now as a man known for his benevolence, the author took a firm line on law and order. He wrote to John Forster on 25 August:

> I cannot easily tell you how much interested I am by what you tell me of our brave and excellent friend the Chief Baron, in connection with that ruffian. I followed the case with so much interest, and have followed the miserable knaves and asses who have perverted it since, with so much indignation, that I have often had more than half a mind to write and thank the upright judge who tried him. I declare to God that I believe such a service one of the greatest that a man of intellect and courage can render to society. Of course I saw the beast of a prisoner (with my mind's eye) delivering his cut and dried speech, and read in every word of it that no one but the murderer could have delivered or conceived it. Of course I have been driving the girls out of their wits here, by incessantly proclaiming that there need to be no medical evidence either way, and that the case was plain without it. Lastly, of course ... I would hang any Home Secretary...who would step in between that black scoundrel and the gallows.

Dickens castigated 'the amiable Smethurst whom the newspapers strangely delight to make a sort of gentleman' and later wrote a pamphlet about the criminal law, in which he stated that reforms be made on the principle 'that the real offender is the Murdered Person'.

Despite Dickens' views, which he appears to have kept private, the Home Secretary, Sir George Cornewell, had Sir Benjamin Bodie, a leading physician, investigate the matter. On 14 November, the Queen was advised to grant Smethurst a free pardon, such were the doubts cast on his conviction, notwithstanding lasting suspicion.

Although Smethurst had escaped the gallows, his troubles were not at an end. He had to return to the Old Bailey yet again, this time on the charge of committing bigamy. This time there was little room for doubt. Witnesses identified both him and his legal wife, and parish clerks read out evidence from the parish registers of Kennington and Battersea. Smethurst was found guilty and he was sentenced to a year's imprisonment.

He may still have been in gaol in early 1861, but later that year, he was once again in court. At least this time, he was not on trial for any offence. He was claiming the money left to him by Isabella Bankes' will of 1859. Louisa Bankes and Mr Tomalin, who was married into the family, contested this on the grounds that he had used undue pressure to make the now deceased sign and that he may have murdered her, too. The case dragged on for a year and it was not until 1862 that the court found in Smethurst's favour. Yet Smethurst only inherited less than £800; possibly not even £200. By now he resided at Hanover Street, Pimlico.

Smethurst returned to his wife in 1862, and she died in Kingston in 1863. Two years later, her husband, now free to marry legitimately, did so, in Denbighshire in 1865, to a woman called Annie, who was twenty-eight (to his sixty). In 1871 the two were living in Scarsdale Terrace (now part of Wright's Avenue, just south of Kensington High Street), Kensington, where he no longer practised medicine in any form, describing himself as 'Householder'. By this time, his brother, William, was again living with them. Smethurst died, of natural causes, on 18 October 1873, aged sixty-eight, in total obscurity, living in a house in Brompton Square. He had under £100 to leave to his widow.

It seems highly probable that Smethurst was innocent of committing murder. It seems likely that Isabella died of irritable bowel syndrome or Crohn's disease. Prejudice may have been built up against him because he was a bigamist, and also because of the suspicions of the medical men. Dr Taylor's initial pronouncement about finding arsenic in one of the bottles, although later taken back, probably also created a negative impression. With the recent high profile poisoning case of Dr Palmer in the public mind, and the fact that Smethurst was a doctor, was another factor against him. And the question of the will in his favour also helped to cause suspicion. Taken together, all these created an apparently strong case against Smethurst. However, the almost certainty that Isabella did not die from arsenic poisoning counters all this and leads us to the conclusion that he was not guilty, so was rightly pardoned.

CHAPTER 4

A Crime of Lunacy 1861

I was reading a newspaper last week and there were accounts of some most dreadful murders in it, and to think that I should be the cause of another!

On Tuesday 26 March 1861, the men of the 3rd Regiment of the Royal Surrey Militia were stationed in their barracks in Kingston. For the married men, such as Sergeant Major Charles Bradish, a forty-year-old, born in London, their wives were also sleeping there. Bradish had enlisted in the 36th Regiment of Foot, the Herefordshire Regiment, in 1850 and served for ten years, before joining his current unit. Next door to the Bradish's room there slept on a sofa Diana Wickens, a woman of twenty years, who was Mrs Martha Bradish's step-sister. Martha had been born in Woolhampton, Berkshire, in about 1816. Miss Wickens had been in domestic service for the last eighteen months, but was now without a place and for the last two weeks had stayed with the Bradishes, which was Mrs Bradish's suggestion, rather than her going to stay with relatives in Berkshire. She was literate and had been seen copying religious tracts.

Bradish left the marital bed at about seven that morning and stepped out into the parade ground. Almost as soon as he had left, his wife, a tall, powerful, plain middle-aged woman, went next door to where her stepsister slept. With her she took one of her husband's razors, which he kept in a drawer in their room.

Shortly afterwards, Sergeant Alexander Oates was crossing the parade ground. He later recalled:

I was going towards the quarters of Sergeant Major Bradish … when I saw Mrs Brandish come out from them very

> excited. She came up to me and said, 'Come in Sergeant Oates; I have murdered my sister'. I observed at this time that the prisoner's hands were covered with blood, and she went to the pump and washed them. Seeing her excited state, and knowing that her husband was not in his quarters, as I had observed him go out a minute or two before, I thought something had happened and I went into the prisoner's room and the first thing I saw was a young woman lying in the floor with her throat cut. I saw her limbs move and she was covered with blood.

Oates immediately left the room and went to find Mrs Bradish's husband and then a doctor. When he returned, the woman, who was only wearing a chemise, and whose name he then did not know, was dead.

Mr Cory, a surgeon, of St James' Road, Kingston, had returned with Oates. It was now just after seven. He later recounted what he saw:

> She was dead, but the flesh was quivering and she was quite warm. I observed a large wound on the right side of her neck, which completely divided the carotid artery, the jugular vein and the windpipe, and on the ring finger on the right hand I also observed a lacerated wound. The prisoner was in the room and when she saw me, she said, 'Oh God, doctor, if I had had your advice before this would never have happened.' I looked around the room to see if I could find any instrument with which the injuries had been inflicted, and then asked the prisoner how she had done it, and she took a razor from a drawer and then handed it to me. It appeared to have been recently washed.

The doctor had seen Mrs Bradish in the previous year, when she was suffering from a diseased liver. He recalled:

> She had been, I believe, in the West Indies, and this had caused the malady from which she was suffering. She was very ill at that time, but she recovered, and I advised her to keep herself quiet and free from excitement.

Mrs Bradish was indeed not a well woman. She had contracted yellow fever whilst she and her husband were in the West Indies in 1857. She suffered from pains in the head and took laudanum for her sleeplessness and had troubled dreams.

PC John Gunner was the first policeman on the scene. Mrs Bradish told him, 'I have cut that young woman's throat and you must take me to the station.' With the arrival of the police, Mrs Bradish was taken to the police station, and Elizabeth Barker, wife of a police sergeant there, searched her. She found some blood on her stocking, apparently caused when Mrs Bradish walked across the room without any shoes on. Sergeant Parsonage received her. He read the charge against her and cautioned her. She was very excited, and on seeing a newspaper, remarked, 'Oh, a newspaper. I was reading a newspaper last week and there were accounts of some most dreadful murders in it, and to think that I should be the cause of another!' Then she said, 'I know where I am. I am in the station house.'

Inspector Armstrong was at the police station at 9am. He entered the charge against her on the police sheet. When he first saw the prisoner, she said, 'This is a shocking thing I have done.' He then cautioned her about saying anything else until she saw a legal representative.

On 26 March, at Kingston Town Hall, the magistrates held court. Mrs Bradish kept interrupting the proceedings by hysterical sobs and emotional shouts. All the time, her husband (never named in newspaper accounts) held her hand. She was committed to trial at the next sitting of the Assizes. Meanwhile, the inquest was held at the *Compasses Inn* in Kingston, two days later and the jury decided that this was a case of murder and that Martha Bradish was responsible.

Martha Bradish was tried at the Home Circuit Assizes, held at Croydon, before Mr Justice Blackburn, on 5 August 1861. She pleaded 'not guilty'. Mr Robinson was the prosecutor and argued that there could be no doubt that Mrs Bradish had struck her step sister a fatal blow. The question, rather, was whether she was responsible for her actions or not. Jealousy nor anger were the motives for the murder. The facts of the murder were then recounted. Medical evidence suggested that

Kingston Town Hall, 1950s. Author's collection

Mrs Bradish had suffered from 'foreign climates' and this might have affected her mental state.

Mr Ribton, for the defence, stated that Mrs Bradish was not responsible for her actions. Witnesses attested to the mental history of her family. Her mother was insane; two relatives had tried to commit suicide and another had succeeded in this. Dr Hood, the consulting physician at the Bethlehem Hospital, an eminent figure in the mental health profession, said that women who were menopausal had been known to act erratically and violence was not unknown.

The jury acquitted the prisoner because she was not sane and so she was ordered to be committed to Broadmoor. Mrs Bradish, who had shown no emotion throughout, was led from the bar and into the asylum for the criminally insane. She clearly was very unwell, both physically and mentally and this led to her violent crime.

Martha Bradish was sent to Broadmoor, but was released on 13 May 1868 and was living in south London in 1871. However, she was readmitted on 21 February 1880. She died there on 14 November 1901. Curiously enough, her husband remarried. By 1881, he was married to one Emily, twenty-five years his junior, and they had a dozen children, aged (in 1881) from one to fourteen. Bradish remained in Kingston as a sergeant major in the militia. Since divorce was almost unknown among the working classes at this time, it is very odd that he remarried in the same locality, even though his first wife was still alive, though in an asylum. He certainly did not divorce his first wife, so the second marriage was illegal. He retired from the Army on 31 January 1883 and was given a strong commendation from his commanding officer, Colonel Daniell. According to Daniell:

> The discharge of Sergeant Major Charles Bradish having been confirmed for this date, the officer commanding cannot allow him to leave the battalion without placing on record the valuable services he has rendered during his connection with the Regiment extending over a period of 22 years and 344 days. In his capacity of Sergeant Major he has uniformly exhibited in a marked degree all the qualifications essential to that position. His exacting energy, impartiality and the cheerful performance of duty under all circumstances however trying, he commanded the respect and ready obedience of all under him and set an example which should be remembered by men of all ranks.

Brandish died in 1890.

CHAPTER 5

Murder or Suicide? 1872

The deceased died from the mortal effects of having her throat cut, but the how the injury was inflicted, there is no evidence to show.

Thomas Martin, an elderly hurdle-maker (he made fences and wooden goods), lived in a two-storey house on the High Street, New Hampton. He had lived there since the 1830s. He was born in Buckinghamshire in about 1786. By 1871, he was a widower, his wife, Frances, dying in the 1860s. They had married in about 1814 and had at least four children. By 1851, all had left the family home, but the eldest, his unmarried daughter, Sarah Hooper Martin, who was aged fifty-two in 1872, had by then returned to live with him and carried on a laundry business on the premises. They were the sole residents.

Not much is known about Sarah. She had worked in domestic service at one time. Currently, she did some charring and sold fish as well as taking in washing. She was very poor and had pledged most of her clothes. Her neighbours knew of her poverty which was something she often complained about. The police report about her character stated that she was, 'a woman of loose habits, and frequently got intoxicated and when she did she got so that she did some very eccentric things'. One of these was to jump out of moving carriages.

On Monday 2 December 1872, Martin returned home at 4 pm and stayed there for an hour. His daughter had company: one Mrs Mitchell and her daughter. Martin then went out for a walk, returning at six. By this time his daughter's visitors had left. It was also said that Sarah James, of North Road, Teddington, saw her, leaving at 6.40. He had his supper and then, just after 7 pm, went upstairs to bed.

As he was retiring for the night, his daughter was entertaining another female guest. The two women seemed to be having an amicable conversation about a place where the two of them had lived together in the past. Martin did not know the strange woman, but thought that she was from Kingston. He didn't know why the woman had come to see Sarah, either. The two stayed together for some time (over two hours). They clearly had a lot to talk about.

Martin did not fall asleep at once. In any case, the sounds he heard below began to occupy his mind. He thought he could hear a scuffling noise, as if chairs and tables were being knocked about and his daughter's voice rang out; or was it a scream? So he called out, 'What's the matter?' He then believed his daughter replied, 'Do you hear me?' When he got out of the bed, he went to the top of the stairs and called out, but heard no reply. Everything was in darkness.

The old man then lit a candle and went downstairs. He found that the front door was open, but no one was about. He assumed that the spring latch had swung open, so he closed the door, fastening it firmly shut. He then went back upstairs to bed. He was not left undisturbed for long. The front door was forced open and a man came up the stairs to see him. It was a police sergeant and he had bad news about his daughter, who he initially said had been taken ill.

It appeared that Sarah and her guest had left the house sometime before 9.40 pm. It was at that latter time that Fanny Nash, a neighbour, heard the sound of something like a chair falling over and Sarah shouting, 'Murder!' She was then indoors. Edward Reddick, a fourteen-year-old plasterer, was actually outside and he heard Sarah shout, 'Police!' and 'Help!' More to the point, he claimed he saw a man jump over the gate of Martin's house and run up the road towards Twickenham. The man was tall, dressed in dark clothes and wore a cap. As a description of a man seen momentarily in the dark, it was not too bad, but as a description of a wanted man it was nigh on useless.

Meanwhile, all attention focussed on Sarah. Mrs Nash had run out into the road, but terrified by Sarah's screams, she quickly went to a nearby beer house, the *Rising Sun*, only

The Rising Sun *pub, 2009.* The Author

returning when others came with her. She then approached Sarah and asked what was amiss. Her neighbour replied, 'Oh! Mrs Nash, I'm murdered.' She then staggered and fell onto the road. By this time, Edward Barnes, the publican of the aforesaid place, had arrived. He later said that Sarah had been briefly into this pub just before 10, and said, 'Oh! Mr Barnes, I'm being murdered.' Barnes did not pay much attention and failed to ask her who was responsible. Sarah then staggered out into the night when Mrs Nash had then seen her.

By this time, David Buckle, a carpenter, and a customer at the *Rising Sun,* had gone over to where Sarah was and picked her up. She said to him, 'For Heaven's sake, take me home.' Finding she was covered with blood, one of the two ran for the police. PC Bassett was quick to arrive and by the time he did so, Sarah was dead. The men took her into her father's house and lay her on the ground floor.

The room was in a state of disarray. Various articles had been disturbed and a plate had been broken. The carpet had been disarranged. Not everything had been knocked over. A glass with a half-pint of beer stood on a table. There was blood on a chair and on the fender. Under the chair was a razor. It was a new one and of an Army pattern. Presumably this was the murder weapon, because Sarah's throat had been cut. Dr Vaughan Holberton, of Hampton, arrived on the scene at about 10 pm. The jagged incised wound was from left to right. The jugular vein had been cut, but it was not deep. There were no other wounds caused by the razor, but her nose had been injured, possibly due to a fall in the road. Certainly her face was smeared with mud, again presumably caused by a fall. No clues could be found outside the house, either.

Dr Diplock, coroner of the Western Division of Middlesex, begun the inquest enquiries at the New Hampton Working Men's Institute. After the doctor and other witnesses had given their evidence, the following conclusion possible was reached: 'The deceased died from the mortal effects of having her throat cut, but how the injury was inflicted, there is no evidence to show'.

Detective Inspector Frederick Williamson and his officers set to work. One possible suspect was John Etherington, a hairdresser, of Richmond, who was a close friend of Sarah's and an occasional visitor, 'who had for many years been intimate with her and from time to time used to give her money'. However, although questioned, 'He admitted that he was in the habit of visiting deceased, but that he had not been to her house for about seven weeks.' He was seen by detectives on the following day and he willingly showed them his clothes and his hands, which were dirty, but there was no sign of any blood there. Moreover, he had a strong alibi. On the night of Sarah's death, he shut up shop at 8.45 pm, then he went to his brother's house at Twickenham, arriving at 9.40 pm. They left twenty minutes later, to meet a friend at *The George* pub. Finally, the three walked home and went as far as Richmond Bridge together. Williamson commented, 'He could not, therefore, if this be true, have been at Hampton at the time of the supposed murder.' The seller of the razor, one Mr Alldiss, of 16 Gray's Inn Road, was unable to help because he could not recall to whom he sold all his wares.

Williamson made his final report on 9 February 1873. He concluded that this was almost certainly a case of suicide, not murder. This was for a number of reasons. Dr Holberton, who examined the corpse, was convinced it was suicide. Secondly, Edward Reddick, who is the only witness to have seen anyone else, was thought to be unreliable, Williamson saying, 'This boy is however known to be dishonest and untruthful, and scarcely any reliance could be placed upon his statement, as he told us two or three different versions to the neighbours.' No evidence for murder existed and there were no signs of a second party or any violence. There seemed, in any case, no reason for anyone to murder her ('we fail at present to obtain any clue to the supposed murderer'), but there were reasons for suicide, given her great poverty. Louisa Digly said, 'The deceased had told her she said she had been very low spirited of late in consequences of being so poor'.

Yet some believed this was murder, and the magistrates were applied to, that they ask the Home Secretary to issue a reward for the apprehension of her killer. *The Times* newspaper also heavily suggested that this was a murder. Yet, as we have seen, in police circles there was 'considerable doubt whether deceased committed suicide or whether she was murdered'. Suicide seems the most likely solution, given the motive; whereas there are none for murder and no second party was ever seen by a reliable witness.

CHAPTER 6

A Pauper's Death
1877

I beg further to report that up to the present time no trace has been obtained of the person or persons supposed to have been concerned in the murder of Patrick Earley.

James Pocock, a large market gardener, of Lower Road, Mortlake, employed a number of men and boys in his gardens. It was his custom to pay his workers on every Saturday evening, and the evening of Saturday 4 August 1877 was no exception. Among those being paid were Patrick Earley, aged about seventy-six, Ernest Burgess and Daniel Lee, all of whom were agricultural labourers. Both Earley and Burgess lived in Lower Road, too, but Lee resided at Sandy Lane in Richmond. Cooper was another worker who was paid at this time. Earley received 15s.

Earley, Cooper and Lee walked along a private road which ran adjacent to the London and South Western Railway on the Mortlake side, past Kew station. Cooper left the other two at this point and went his separate way home. The two others continued, but finding his pace was slowed by the old man's walk, Burgess left him and proceeded rather more quickly. He was doubtless surprised to see on his walk a man who he knew worked as a labourer for a Mr Morrison. Thinking nothing of this, he continued his walk home.

However, on Monday morning, George Frampton, foreman at Pocock's gardens, noticed Earley's absence. He seems to have been the first person to have made a fuss about this. Fearing that the old man had had a fit, Pocock instituted a search for him. Burgess told him of the last time he had seen Earley alive. Lee looked in a large plantation of gooseberry bushes, where, on their outside, he saw a gathering basket amongst them, about twenty yards from the path where Burgess and Earley had

Lower Richmond Road, 2009. The Author

walked along on the preceding Saturday. It was the type of basket that women put fruit in and were sometimes left behind. He went over towards it and amongst the bushes made a shocking discovery. He saw Earley's body.

He was lying on his right side, across two gooseberry bushes. His body was drawn up and his left arm was partially raised as if he had tried to defend himself. His head was hanging down and beneath it was a round hole, full of blood.

It was a secluded place. To have reached it would have meant to have left the path and then turning into a path across the gardens which led to a row of walnut trees. The path then turned to the right and was secluded and shady. It was assumed that he had been stunned near to the path and then carried to the spot where he was murdered. There were no signs of broken bushes or any indication of a struggle having occurred. There was no reason why anyone should have gone to that site, as the gathering season was over. It could have lain there for months before being spotted. Once it had been found, however, the alarm was raised.

Mr George Cundell, a surgeon, of Kew, was the doctor who was called. He thought that Earley had been dead for two days. Decomposition had already set in. There was severe bruising on the left forearm and hand and a slight puncture between the thumb and finger. There was a large wound to the left hand side of the face. Death had been caused by having his throat cut. A sharp instrument had been used here, but the other injuries may have been caused by a boot. There were also four scalp wounds, inflicted by the same sharp weapon which was used for the throat cutting. Earley had probably been rendered unconscious, then killed in the secluded spot, as well as being stamped upon. The body was then removed to the mortuary.

Sergeant George Clarke was the first policeman on the site. He went through the deceased's pockets. In them he found an old pocket knife, five raw potatoes and a clay pipe. In another pocket was an old pipe and two sixpences. On the ground near to the corpse was a hat, which had a cut in it. There was also a handkerchief. Finally, a piece of cord was found on a nearby branch, and this was bloodstained. The cord was of a type used by women in gathering fruit and probably had no connection with the man's death. Despite a search by two constables, nothing else could be found.

On Thursday 9 August, at the *Queen's Head,* Mortlake, the inquest commenced. There were also police, journalists and spectators present, too. Daniel Lee, who had made the grisly discovery, was the first to give evidence. He recounted his activities on that Monday morning. He left home at 6am and, having collected his tools, got to work and carried on until 8am. He then returned home for breakfast. By this time he had been told about Earley's disappearance, so he decided to look among the gooseberry bushes, because he had been last reported as being seen in that vicinity.

The adjourned inquest took place on Friday 17 August. The police stated that they had been following one lead, but it had led nowhere. However, they now had a more promising lead. They believed that the killer might have been a man employed by Mr Morrison, at the *Bee Hive* pub, who had disappeared on the day of the murder, though he had not been discharged and was expected to turn up to work on the following Monday. Morrison remembered paying the man 7s 6d on the Saturday evening, before leaving. The man may have had a small handled hoe in his bag, but was not carrying the tools he worked with: a long handled hoe and a spade. He was not named in public, but the following description was issued to every police station in the country:

> Age forty-five, height five feet nine inches, square shoulders, proportionate build, dark complexion, dark brown hair (inclined to curl), beard, whiskers and thick moustache (long), dark and peculiar eyes, dressed in dark pilot jacket and vest, dirty fustian trousers (large patch on one knee), black billy cock hat, heavy lace boots. Carried a thin canvas or hempen skeleton bag, containing a coat similar to one worn. Works as an excavator or gardener's labourer, and is known as 'Jim'. Information to be sent to Superintendent Williamson, Detective Department, Scotland Yard.

It was thought that the killer was a married man and the description of his wife was thus:

> His wife, a short, stout, dark woman, wearing a hat with a thick full supposed to reside in Hammersmith.

This man had been seen by Burgess as he walked home on Saturday night, and whom Burgess vaguely knew by sight greeted him with a 'good night, mate'. Presumably he attacked Earley shortly afterwards.

The inquest was then wound up with the predictable verdict brought by the jury that this was murder by an unknown assailant. Despite the Home Office offering a reward, no one was ever charged with the offence and the man whose description is noted above was never apprehended.

It is obscure why anyone should want to kill Earley, about whom little is known. There is a man of that name in the 1871 census; he is said to have been a labourer, born in Ireland in 1803, so this matches with what we know of him. Furthermore, in 1871, he was living in Glossop, Derbyshire, was married to one Bridget and they then had five children living with them. If this is our man, then presumably his wife had died between 1871–77 and he had moved south to look for work. He was of small height and was described as being quiet and inoffensive. He spent the summers working as a gardener, lodging with John William's family at Garden Row, Mortlake, and spending the winters in Richmond Workhouse. His only known kin was Mary Welsh, an elderly and almost blind inmate of the forementioned workhouse, who was his sister. He liked his drink and had been before the Richmond magistrates on a couple of times for drunkenness, but apart from that had no history of trouble with the law. He usually ran up a 'slate' of between four and five shillings a week at the *Beehive*, by consuming about eight pence of tobacco and drink each evening, before paying it back on payday.

He was buried at Mortlake Cemetery on Thursday 9 August, at 6 pm. As with many other murder victims, a large crowd turned out, between 200-300 people. Although he was a Catholic, for some reason he was buried in the Protestant part of the cemetery and there was a rumour that there might be a disturbance because of this. Thus police were present, but apart from 'a slight outbreak from an Irishman present', there was no trouble. Since the deceased was a pauper, the expense of the funeral fell on the council.

As well as not knowing who killed Earley, it is unknown why he should have been killed. Perhaps the killer had a secret grudge against him; perhaps he was killed for the small amount of money he had on him after being paid his wages; perhaps the killer had what police would have then termed 'homicidal tendencies'. The police thought that the financial motive was the right one, with Inspector Edward Sayer writing, 'The motive being the obtaining of his weekly wages and an additional sum he was entitled to for piece work … just before his last being seen alive [he] was heard to boast of the amount of money due to him.'

Strenuous efforts were made to apprehend the killer. There were 2,500 handbills describing the killer distributed to police stations throughout the country. There was also an advert in the *Police Gazette*, an official police newspaper. On 21 August, a reward of £100 was offered for the killer's arrest. Many suspects were identified. On 9 August, one John Johnson, aged thirty-three and from Mansfield, Nottinghamshire, was arrested in Worcester for vagrancy. He answered the description in some ways, but not all. He was five feet six inches, with dark brown hair and a thick moustache and blue eyes. He also worked as a gardener's labourer. Crucially, though, he was not the right height.

On 16 August, there was a report of a man seen in Watford and Luton who looked like the killer. On the following day, in Escrick, in the East Riding, George Appleby, a gardener, was arrested for vagrancy. He was five feet seven inches, with blue eyes and red hair. He had once worked in London and at Kew Gardens. He was discounted when Mr Morrison and his wife went up to see him and did not identify him.

George Wyse was another man suspected, but again was excluded after he had been seen. The Morrisons accompanied Sayer to many places, including Hampshire, Hertfordshire and London to see men who were seen as potential suspects, and all this cost them considerable time and money, as Sayer reported on 17 October. The problem was that it was all too late. Sayer noted that it had been forty-eight hours between the murder and the discovery of the body. Given that the killer was 'supposed to be a man without any fixed habitation and a perfect stranger to the neighbourhood', to leave the locality without attracting any suspicion was straightforward.

The police conclusion was a depressing one: 'I beg further to report that up to the present time no trace has been obtained of the person or persons supposed to have been concerned in the murder of Patrick Earley.'

Nothing else was ever heard of in connection with the case.

CHAPTER 7

Murdered and Chopped Up 1879

One of the most dangerous classes in the world is the drifting and friendless woman. She is the most harmless, and often the most useful of mortals, but she is the inevitable inciter of crime in others ... She is a stray chicken in a world of foxes – Sherlock Holmes

This chapter concerns the least unknown story in the book – both brutal and macabre. Perhaps the key character is Mrs Julia Martha Thomas. Born in St James', Piccadilly, in about 1824, she was twice married; firstly to one Mr Murray, whom she was widowed by 1851, and then to James Thomas. Thomas was a printer's reader and the couple lived in Finsbury in 1871, at Melbourne Terrace, then at Hazelville Road, Hornsey Lane. Two years later, on 28 June 1873, her second husband had followed the first one to the grave (he left just under £1,500 to her in his will). They had had no children, or at least none who survived infancy. Such a high rate of mortality among both adults and, especially children, was not uncommon at the time. Charles Menhennick, of Ambler Road, Finsbury, was a friend and described her thus:

> Mrs Thomas was an amiable, good natured sort of lady – she was about 55 or 56 years of age – she was not stout, she was animated in her manner and appeared reasonably strong – she was not an invalid, she was an ordinary person ... she played the piano well.

She also enjoyed a little work in the garden, attending chapel and was comfortably off. She was about five feet four in height. It is not certain what she did after her second husband's death, but by March 1877 she was living in salubrious Richmond, at

Townshend Road, 2009. The Author

Mary Ann Kent's house, in St Mary's Villas (now part of Townshend Road). She left in April 1878. She then put an advert in a newspaper, reading, 'A lady wished to meet with an elderly or widow lady to join in taking a house, at once in Richmond: companionship desired; willing to let rooms not required; could furnish in part; references exchanged. J.T.' She was unsuccessful, so briefly rented a house in St Mary's Grove, Richmond.

In September 1878, she leased for seven years a semi-detached cottage called 2 Vine Cottages, later renamed Mayfield and now 9 Park Road, from Miss Elizabeth Ives, who lived with her widowed mother, Jane, at number 1. The house was described thus, 'a small but very respectable house, and its appearance would suggest that it is the dwelling of a person in good circumstances'. Ironically the street was only two streets parallel to that where Isabella Bankes died twenty years previously. She did not see much of her neighbours, with Jane Ives remarking, 'I did not know Mrs Thomas personally, I knew there was a lady of that name living next door'. Mrs Thomas

Vine Cottages, Park Road, 2009. The Author

did not have any close friends in Richmond, only a number of acquaintances, and this worked to her disadvantage.

At first she had the thirteen-year-old Edith, daughter of Mr Menhennick, live with her. At the end of January 1879 she decided she needed a 'proper' servant. A respectable local dressmaker knew of a charwoman. This was one Katherine Webster. She had been born in Enniscorthy, Wexford, Ireland in about 1850, and was a tall, strong woman, built like a navvy, as one observer noted. She told Mrs Thomas that she had been in laundry work in Hammersmith, but preferred a change.

Regrettably, Mrs Thomas did not ask for character references, then usual for anyone engaging someone as a domestic servant who was unknown to them. First of all, she lied about her former address; she was living in Kingston, not Hammersmith. She also had an illegitimate son, aged five, born in Kingston Workhouse in April 1873, and whose father (one Mr Strong) lived in Kingston. More importantly, Katherine had a long criminal record. She had been in trouble with the law in Ireland and had been gaoled in 1867. Travelling to England, she persisted in her criminal career. On 4 May 1875 she was convicted at the Surrey Quarter Sessions for thirty-six robberies in the Kingston district, and was given a gaol sentence in Wandsworth prison of eighteen months. The gaol sentence failed to act as a deterrent, for on her release, she returned to her old life. Again, she was unsuccessful and on 6 February 1877 she was once again brought before the magistrates in Surrey; and was sentenced to twelve months for felony. She went by a number of aliases, her surname being variously Gibbs, Webb, Shannon and Lawler. Her activities in the next eleven months after her release are unknown, though we know she was working as a charwoman in Richmond at the beginning of 1879. She may have worked as a servant in Teddington.

Katherine began working and living with Mrs Thomas on 28 January 1879 (her son was then living in Eccles Road, Richmond). We do not know much of life in the cottage or how the two women related to each other, but it is thought that Mrs Thomas soon realised she did not like living with

Katherine and wanted to have a more amenable companion in the house. By the end of February, matters were not looking good. On 28 February, Mrs Thomas wrote in her diary (on the day that her servant had her monthly holiday, spent at Kingston with her son's father), 'Gave Katherine warning to leave'. This may have been on account of her servant's drinking habits. Two days later, on Sunday 2 March, Mrs Thomas went to the Presbyterian service held at the Lecture Hall on Hill Street. She went both in the morning and again in the evening.

Julia Nichols, a servant, also attended the same evening service and remembered seeing Mrs Thomas there, and behaving oddly. Apparently, 'she came late, and did not occupy her usual seat. She made a statement to me, and was very excited.' Mrs Thomas left at 7.30 pm. It would have taken her about fifteen minutes to walk home.

On the following morning, Katherine was hard at work, washing clothes and hanging them out to dry. The copper (the laundry tub) was much in use. There were two callers for Mrs Thomas that day, but neither were able to see her. Firstly, William Dean, a coal agent called, but Katherine only opened the front door sufficiently enough for him to see her face. He asked her if Mrs Thomas was in, and when he was told she was not, he asked when she might return. Katherine abruptly told him she didn't know when this would be. Mary Roberts, apprentice to her neighbour, called to tell her that a man would be coming to fix the roof at Mrs Thomas' request, but Katherine told her this would no longer be necessary. She did not open the door, but spoke from an upper window.

Katherine went to visit some of the Porters, who were old friends of hers, in Hammersmith, on the morning of Tuesday 4 March. In about 1873 she had lodged in a house on Rose Gardens (later renamed Cardoss Street), and had become friendly with the Porter family, but after a few months she had moved to Norland Crescent in Notting Hill, though she occasionally visited them until the end of the year and they had never seen nor heard from her until this day. Katherine told Mrs Porter, who was at home, that she had married a Mr Thomas, who had since died. It also seemed to Mrs Porter that her old friend had done well for herself, for she was wearing expensive clothes and jewellery.

But because her husband, Henry, a painter employed by Mr Bird of Hammersmith, was out at work, as was Robert, her fifteen-year-old son, Katherine promised to return that evening when all the family would be at home. She did so, travelling by train, when it was quite dark, carrying a heavy black bag, weighing between 40-50 pounds. Katherine also explained that her aunt, who had lived at Richmond was dead and her father had told her to sell the house's contents. She asked if they could help her with her bag as far as Hammersmith Bridge. They did so, and parted at the *Oxford and Cambridge* pub, via *The Angel* in King Street. At the former pub, the Porters had refreshment. After a short time, Katherine parted with them, whilst she went towards the bridge, returning shortly, without her bag.

She then asked if she could have the services of Robert, because she needed more help with her belongings in Richmond. The Porters consented, on condition that he returned home that night. The two went to Park Road. Leaving Robert standing outside, Katherine was some time in finding what she needed. Eventually she returned with a box, tied up with cord. It was now 11 pm and very dark. She said to the lad, 'Here Bob, I want you to help me with this to the other side of the bridge.' It was about three quarters of a mile to Richmond

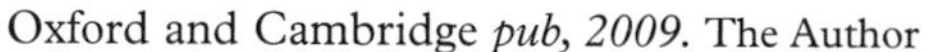
Oxford and Cambridge *pub, 2009.* The Author

Bridge and they slowly walked there, taking time to rest when needed. On arriving there, she told him, 'Now Bob, you run back – I'll soon catch you. I've to meet a friend there.' They had already walked half way across the bridge, so she did not have to carry the box by herself very far. The night was dark, it was a lonely place which the boy did not know, so he stayed where he was. He then heard a loud splash. Robert and a passing man both peered over the bridge into the Thames, the latter remarking, 'A barge, I suppose.'

Katherine was soon once more at Robert's side, and took him by the arm, saying, 'Come along, Bobby, I've seen my friend, and I've left the box.' By this time, it was too late to take the last train back to Hammersmith, so the two went back to Park Road. Robert did not want to go with her and wanted to take a cab back home, but did not have enough money. She talked to the boy between 1 and 2 am, giving him rum to drink and drinking alcohol herself. She made him a bed on the kitchen floor. Then, later that morning, Robert caught a train back to Hammersmith.

Later that week, Katherine went back to her friends at Hammersmith. She explained to them that she needed to sell the house's furniture, telling them that the house belonged to her aunt, but there was to be no public auction there. She needed someone who would agree to buy the furniture there. Porter introduced her to one John Church, a former soldier

Cardross Road, 2009. The Author

Hammersmith Bridge, 2009. The Author

and a married man, who was publican of *The Rising Sun* in Hammersmith. It seemed that neither had met before. The three of them went to the house on Park Road several times in the next few days, driving around Richmond in cabs and spending not a little time in public houses, such as *The Talbot* and *The King's Head*. Church and Katherine were thought to have been very friendly towards one another. Mrs Thomas' neighbours found all this activity rather peculiar, especially as some of it happened late at night in this normally quiet residential street.

Katherine and Church came to an agreement that he would pay her £68 for the furniture and goods, giving her £18 on account. The day for the removal of these items, which included iron bedsteads, carpets, chairs, looking glasses, book cases, sofa, couch and other household goods, was Tuesday 18 March. Church brought a van around with some workmen. Mrs Ives made enquiries, 'What are you doing with those goods? The workmen explained that they were taking them away to be sold. She then said, 'You cannot take the goods. Mrs Thomas has taken the house for a term of years, and we are the owners. Where is Mrs Thomas?' The men asked for Katherine, who, not suspecting the nature of their enquiry, came into Mrs Ives' vision. Mrs Ives addressed her, 'This is very strange moving your mistress' goods. Where is Mrs Thomas?' This puzzled the workmen, who had been led to believe that Katherine was Mrs Thomas. Katherine told Miss Ives, 'Mrs Thomas has sold the things and this man can show you the receipt. Mr Westcomb is to take them to Hammersmith.' She was evasive about where Mrs Thomas was.

Katherine did not stay around for much longer. That day she returned to the Porter's house, where she had left her son a few days ago. Taking him and borrowing a guinea from Mrs Porter, they took a cab to Hammersmith station and then a train from there to King's Cross station. They then travelled from there by train to Liverpool and on 21 March the two reached Enniscorthy in Ireland. She announced that she was the widow of Captain John Webster and that she had lost four children.

Meanwhile, other discoveries of a disturbing nature were being found near Richmond, though at first no connection was made between them and Katherine Webster. On 5 March, Henry Wrigley, of Mortlake, a coal porter, was walking by the towpath near Barnes. He saw an unusual sight, as he later recalled:

> I saw a box in the Thames about 6.45 am on Wednesday, March 5, on the lower side of Barnes Bridge – the tide was not ebbing from the top of it – it was half afloat – it had a cord twice around it, across – I kicked it and broke it to pieces – the handle was off, I believe – I went to the station and fetched someone, leaving a man named Kerrison in charge of it ... before I went I saw a lot of what looked like cooked meat inside it – it was quite full.

PS Tomas Childs arrived to take charge of the box, and he reported that the contents of the box seemed to be human remains, each piece wrapped in brown paper. Clearly murder had been committed. He called Dr Adams, of Barnes, who briefly examined them. He concluded that these mutilated remains belonged to a woman aged between twenty and thirty, judging by the brown hair on an armpit. The CID and the divisional police were informed and a search was made along the Thames near Barnes to see if anyone was missing. It transpired that a young German woman employed as a servant had recently left her post in East Sheen and had not been seen since. She was also known to have had a box like the one in which the human remains had been found. This supported Dr Adams' theory about the age of the victim. There was an inquest at the *Red Lion Hotel* on 10 March, which was adjourned for a week.

Other body parts were found in the following days. On 12 March, Edward Shaw found the remains of a human foot in a dung pile and two weeks later the police found a carpet bag with burnt bones, a chopper and female clothing. However, no head was ever found and the body was never definitely identified, as is the case when a body is chopped up and never wholly located – there was a similar case in 1873 when parts of a female body was found in the Thames (detailed in the author's *Unsolved Murders in Victorian and Edwardian London*).

Eventually, Thomas Bond, a lecturer in forensic science who was also employed at Westminster Hospital, was brought to the mortuary to see the remains (in 1888 he examined a number of the victims of Jack the Ripper). He made a rather more thorough examination and came to radically different conclusions than Dr Adams. He concluded that the remains were those of a short middle-aged woman, and that the body had been sawn into pieces by someone with no anatomical skill.

Meanwhile, on 19 March, Church returned to Park Road and tried to talk to Miss Ives, but she slammed the door in his face. In the meantime, the clothing taken from the house was examined by Church. He found a letter addressed to Mrs Thomas from her friends, the Menhennicks, in Finsbury, whom he informed on 21 March, as well as telling them about his dealings with Katherine. They passed this information onto Mr Hughes, Mrs Thomas' solicitor. Hughes made enquiries in Richmond and was told that this client of his had not been seen for three weeks and there had been great commotion in the house in the past weeks. He contacted Inspector John Pearman of the Richmond Police, who was already investigating the case of the human remains found in the box in the Thames. He became very suspicious.

Pearman and Hughes found out about Church and searched his premises on 22 March, finding rings belonging to the missing woman, as identified by the Menhennicks. Church told them about his transaction with Katherine. That same day they then went to Mrs Thomas' house, and were given access by Miss Ives. Leaving Porter and Church outside, the other two entered. Pearman later explained:

> We found everything in great confusion – the furniture packed up, and bed linen and wearing apparel packed up in three large boxes, which corded. The carpets were up in the three back bedrooms, while the dining room and drawing room carpets were partly turned up at the sides of the rooms. There was no one in the house.

Some of Mrs Thomas' jewellery was found in the house. Next day, the police heard Robert Porter's tale of helping Katherine with a box. On 24 March, Pearman returned to Park Road. He went to the basement to search the scullery and the kitchen and made a number of sinister discoveries, as he explained:

> I searched the ashes under the kitchen grate and found a quantity of charred bones and some burnt buttons of a woman's dress … I found more charred bones, these being in the copper furnace … taking the copper out of the brick work, I found, half way down, a fatty substance adhering to the sides … I found what appeared to be a bloodstain on the wainscot of the room called the long bedroom.

He took samples of his finds away, and also found a chopper and a knife, but not a saw. He also found Mrs Thomas' diary with a comment about giving her servant notice to leave.

Furthermore, a letter was found addressed to Katherine from her friends in Ireland, giving their address – so the police now knew where to go to find her.

Inspector John Dowdell was despatched to Ireland to apprehend Katherine Webster. He was joined by Inspector Jones and together they made their way from Dublin to Wexford. She had been detained by one William Roche of the Irish police already and on 28 March he had the wanted woman in his custody. He told her she would be charged with murder, but she did not reply. Mr Robinson, a magistrate there, made out a warrant for her to be committed to Richmond magistrates. Her uncle, a small farmer, did not accept her son, so he was committed to Enniscorthy workhouse. The two policemen went back to England with their prisoner by ferry to Holyhead. She said to him, 'Is there any other person in custody for the murder?' They did not reply, so she added, 'There ought to be; the innocent should not suffer for the guilty.'

Her story concerned Church, whom she said she had known for seven years and was seeing a great deal of. He talked of killing Mrs Thomas and selling her goods. On 3 March she said he visited the house and Katherine left. On her return she said she saw Mrs Thomas dying, having been stabbed to death by Church, who threatened to do the same to her if she breathed a word to anyone. In subsequent days they disposed of the body and began to sell the goods. The police seemed to have been impressed with the story.

The magistrates in Richmond began to examine the case in the Vestry Hall on 31 March. There was great local excitement about this case and crowds gathered around, but few could gain admittance into the court room. Katherine was described thus:

> The woman was pale, but she was firm and self possessed, with no trace of excitement in her demeanour. She has no characteristics of a criminal in her face, and, though not handsome, is not ill-looking. Her jacket was of shabby cloth, trimmed with imitation fur, and her dress of the material and cut usually favoured by respectable servants. Her hat was stylish and out of keeping with a servant's position.

She was charged with murder and robbery, but because of her statement to Pearman, Church was also accused. The hearings at Richmond continued for several days as all the witnesses gave evidence. The case of the prosecution was that Mrs Thomas was last seen alive on 2 March, and that Katherine had killed her on that day. She had then boiled down the body, chopped it into pieces, and had packed it up. On 4 March she enlisted the help of the Porters to try and dispose of the body in the Thames. This had only been partially successful, for although the remains in the bag had not been found, and never were, those in the other box were enough. She then proceeded to sell the dead woman's belongings.

Eventually, Church was cleared of all charges because nothing could be found to substantiate any of the claims made against him by Katherine. She, however, was committed for trial at the Old Bailey. She had remained calm and resolute throughout the whole proceedings. She was sent to Clerkenwell gaol in the meantime. As with the examinations in Richmond, the case at the Old Bailey in July proceeded for several days. Her defence argued that there was no definite proof that the human remains found in the river were those of Mrs Thomas, and if she could not have been proved to have been deceased, Katherine could not be charged with her murder. It was also said that even if they were her remains, there was no way of knowing how she had met her death – it could have been

Vestry Hall Magistrates' Court, 2009. Author's collection

Richmond Bridge, 1900s. Author's collection

accidental, not murder. A witness gave evidence of Katherine's good character, a woman stating how 'loving and motherly' she was towards her little son. Yet, the weight of the evidence was such that Katherine was found guilty and so sentenced to death. She then claimed she was pregnant, but upon investigation this was found to be untrue.

She was sent to Wandsworth prison on 8 July, a gaol she had been detained at in previous years. As a Catholic, Father McEnery saw her on the night before her execution. She then told him that she had a confession to make to the prison governor, Captain Colvill. Katherine told him what happened on 2 March at 2 Vine Cottages:

> I alone committed the murder of Mrs Thomas. I was slightly excited by having taken some drink, and when my mistress came home I was aggravated by her manner. I pushed her downstairs and then strangled her.

On Tuesday 29 July, at 9am, inside Wandsworth prison, Katherine Webster was hanged by the neck until she was dead. An inquest was carried out on her body, and then she was buried within the prison, quicklime being poured into her coffin.

There is a story recounted by Henry Mayhew, a journalist and social reformer, who had had a conversation with a street urchin. The lad had told him that Katherine had distributed jars of dripping and bread in Wandsworth in recent times. There is reason to doubt this story, because Katherine spent her time away from work with her son or/and his father in Kingston, so would have not had had the time to have indulged in charitable works, and nothing in her known character suggests she was that way inclined. There is also a much repeated story that Katherine hawked around jars of dripping made from late employer, in Richmond, but there is no evidence to support this ghastly tale.

This crime was of great interest to the reading public of the time. This was for several reasons. Firstly, it was plain murder, and that was always reported in detail. Secondly, the victim was middle class, which was unusual, because most violent deaths were the lot of the poor. Thirdly, the victim was, unusually, mutilated after death. Finally, because this was a murder by a servant of her mistress – not unknown – as seen, in 1812 two French aristocrats were killed by their servant, but very rare. Most middle-class people in this period had at least one servant, and for them to be murdered by one who was lowly, seemed terrible and unnatural, as if the whole social system was being turned on its head.

The actual mechanics of the murder are simple enough. Katherine Webster can almost be described as a career criminal, though this was her first violent crime. It seems she probably drank and this, unsurprisingly offended her employer. Being told to leave was probably the final straw. Whether she planned to kill her employer for what she could steal or whether the thought only occurred after the murder (motivated by anger at the loss of her place), is hard to know. After the murder, she disposed of the body and then set about making money from the dead woman's goods. Yet, as with her previous criminal endeavours, she did not handle them very competently and gave herself away – part of the body being found and Miss Ives seeing her try to masquerade as Mrs Thomas. A swift investigation by Hughes and the police soon wormed out the truth and had her tracked down. After that, her end was near.

This murder is now known only to students of crime, but in 1879 it was a *cause celebre* for the reasons mentioned above.

Chapter 8

Murdered Whilst on Duty 1881

We are almost hopeless of ever being able to bring this crime home to the person who committed the murder.

The life of the Victorian policeman was not always pleasant. Long hours, low pay, physical danger, few days off and being sneered at by writers of detective fiction were among its negative aspects. As *The Pirates of Penzance* puts it, their 'lot is not a happy one'. For some officers, it could be fatal, and whilst one might think that police work would be more dangerous among the inner city slums, it could also be lethal in the affluent suburbs, too.

Burglaries in the larger houses in Kingston had been common in the autumn of 1881. There had been a burglary at The Woodlands, Kingston Hill, on Monday night of 19 September 1881. The bedroom of a servant was entered via a ladder and money and a little jewellery was taken. On the following day, two men were seen leaving a house called Coombe Leigh with a silver box. No one was hurt in either of these two incidents.

PC Frederick Atkins was only twenty-three and had been in the police force for four and a half years (joining on 14 May 1877). His beat began at 10 pm. In the early hours of Thursday 22 September 1881, he was on his beat on Kingston Hill. One of the detached houses which stood on this road was The Knoll (on the east side of the road, now demolished), then the residence of the wealthy Mr Powys-Keck. It was a lonely spot. His household servants included William Short, the butler, James Bloomfield, valet and Harriet Snow, the housekeeper.

On the previous evening, Short locked up just before 11. Everything seemed to be then safe, as he went to bed himself. Yet at about 1.40am, the household was roused by a number of loud noises just outside the building. Short left his bed and stood at the landing. His fellow servants had also heard the noises and were coming up the stairway to meet him. A search of the house revealed nothing amiss, but when they reached the hall door, they heard a moan.

Opening the door, Short saw a policeman lying on the ground. His helmet was at his feet and he was evidently in great pain. Short sent a footman to go to the police station for help. No one else was in the vicinity, but near to the prone figure was a 'dark' (unlit) lantern, they also found a screwdriver and a jemmy. Short stayed with the injured man, not taking him indoors because he thought he was having a fit. Bloomfield helped move him to a more comfortable position and gave him some water. On removing the man's tunic they discovered he had not suffered a fit, but had been seriously injured, so they then rebuttoned the tunic. Underneath him was a broomstick.

It was some time (half an hour) before help arrived, and when it did there was a further wait for a doctor. Inspector Henry Rushbridge, who had ridden on horseback from Kingston police station to the scene, asked his injured colleague, who was PC Atkins, 'What is the matter, Atkins? Have there being burglars here?' He said, faintly, 'I don't know, sir.' When Dr Roots, the divisional surgeon, appeared on the scene he concluded that Atkins was dying. He had been wounded in three places – the chest, the groin and the abdomen. Furthermore, his hands and face were icy. There were no burn marks on the man's tunic, so the shots had not been fired at very close range. He was conveyed to the police station in London Road. It was not thought that in his weakened condition, he should be moved to Surbiton Cottage Hospital, which was further away. The Reverend Father Morey, a local Catholic priest, did his best to administer to Atkins, but the constable was unable to comprehend what was going on.

Kingston Police station, 2009. The Author

Meanwhile, inspectors Bond, Rushbridge and Crowther were despatching constables to secure any suspects found in the vicinity of Kingston Hill. Yet no one could be found and there was no clue to their identity. Footprints were found, but they only led to Richmond Park, whereafter they could not be traced. It seemed, eventually, that only one man had been involved. Although a man was soon arrested, it was just as quickly learnt that he had nothing to do with the burglary and murder and so was released.

This individual was Frank Brockwell, a farrier, of London Road, who lived not far from the Knoll. It is not certain why he was first suspected, but the police visited him on the morning of the crime. They found that his boots matched the footprints found near to the Knoll. He was detained at Norbiton and held for seven hours. On the previous evening he had been drinking at the *Railway Tavern*, Coombe Lane, until about 11 pm. He had then gone home, had supper, gone to bed and had not left home since. His story was accepted and was allowed to go free.

It was obvious enough that Atkins had disturbed a burglar. The tools already mentioned as being found by the house indicated that was the case. Furthermore, it was noted that a bar from a small window leading to a lavatory near the front of the mansion had been removed. Clearly Atkins had interrupted their operations and that was why he was shot whilst they were escaping. Atkins could not tell much, because when he was on his rounds near the house, he had neither heard nor seen anything before he was shot. In any case, in the early hours of Friday 23 September, Atkins died of his wounds. One of the bullets had pierced his lungs.

There was great public concern over what had happened, though whether it was due to shock at the constable's death or worry that murderous burglars were in the neighbourhood, it is not possible to discern. One newspaper noted:

> The quiet neighbourhood of Kingston on Hill was early yesterday morning thrown into a state of excitement by the perpetration of another of those desperate outrages by

Walton-on-Thames church, 1900s. Author's collection

> burglars on the police which of late years have startled the public of the metropolis and the provinces.

A reward of £200 was advertised for the apprehension of the killer.

The inquest was held on Saturday 24 September, at *The Clarence Arms*, Kingston. Atkins' relatives, principally John Atkins, a postman, identified the body and then the coroner for Mid-Surrey adjourned the hearing for another week. He did, however, allow the family to remove the corpse to Walton-on-Thames for burial. This took place at the parish church on Thursday 29 September. It was very well attended. Superintendent Digby and eleven inspectors from V division were there, as were 1,500 other police officers from various parts of London. Members of the local fire brigades also turned out to pay their respects, as did many local people. Shops were shut on the day of the funeral as a mark of respect. The funeral procession was followed by the police band playing the Dead March from Saul.

The murder investigation was led by Howard Vincent and two other detectives from the division. Additional clues were that the killer had fled towards the main road first, before going to the Park. The screwdriver had the initials GB on it, which were those of G Bessell, of Commercial Road, East London, but none of this design had been made since 1876. Enquiries to the maker were not helpful. The revolver used in the crime was a six barrel, .450 bore. There was some question as to why Atkins should have left his beat to go up to the private house. Did he see something suspicious? Did the house's owner pay him to keep a look out on his house? The answer was that the Commissioner had given orders that the house be kept a special eye on.

Another witness was William Brown, the lodge keeper at The Knoll, who recalled being awoken from his sleep by the opening of the gate and from his window he saw the flashing of a bull's eye lantern. This would have been Atkins. Brown then heard someone cry 'All right'. Brown returned to his bed and remained there until after Atkins had been shot and one of his fellow servants told him what had happened. He then went up to the house and saw Short and Bloomfield with Atkins. Apparently the dying man made a number of remarks to those assembled: 'I saw no one', 'I heard no one', 'I was coming to the house when fired at', 'I saw no one about on my beat and 'I heard no one run away'.

The adjourned inquest was concluded at *The Clarence Arms* on 3 October, and the witnesses told how they found the victim, and then the police officials and doctors spoke of what they found. Digby concluded that, despite all their efforts, and an increased reward of £300, there was very little chance that the perpetrator would be caught:

> I am desired to explain the extreme difficulties which we labour in this case and to say that in the absence of any evidence, direct or indirect, entering upon the tragedy, also in the absence of any marks either upon the chisel or on the lantern, we are almost hopeless of ever being able to bring this crime home to the person who committed the murder ... The large reward may lead to something tangible, but as yet we have not a single thing to work on.

The jury found that this was a case of 'murder by person or persons unknown'. He was never found, whoever he was. It was supposed that he was a local burglar, who had committed other offences, but only one with such fatal consequences.

There were a few letters to the local press about this murder. All had different angles. One was shocked at the seeming inhumanity of the servants of the house who did not take the wounded man inside in order to relieve his sufferings, 'such unkind disregard shown to an individual who among all others was most deserving of commendation' should be noted.

Another was a concerned householder, who pointed out the shortcomings of the police. He thought that the notable fact which had hitherto been overlooked was that ordinarily one PC Kavanagh would have been on the beat which on the fatal night had been Atkins' lot. The writer noted that Kavanagh had been on duty at a race meeting at Hampton on the previous day so had not been allotted to the beat in question. He thought that the burglar would have been aware of this fact. He also thought that the burglar must have been casing the joint hitherto because he seemed to know where a possible entry might be affected. Another pointer to the fact that this burglary was carefully planned was that the palings around the grounds were potentially highly dangerous and so the man probably found a safe exit in advance of his expedition. He hoped the police would look further into the matter.

The third letter writer was rather more positive towards the police. He recalled that there had been an attempt to burgle his house one night two years ago. He also noted another occasion, when he shot at the burglar (such practices were not officially frowned upon then), and four police officers arrived on the spot in record time, even though his house was fairly isolated. He concluded, 'I address you in the hope that it will be satisfactory to the local force to show them that their efforts and willingness to aid are truly appreciated in this neighbourhood.'

The local press concluded with the following observation on the matter:

> We were quite prepared to hear that the police were hopeless of ever being able to bring the murderer to justice. The police, perhaps, have never had any case to investigate in which there has been as little ground to work upon as in this; but it is to be hoped, that although public excitement in reference to this tragedy is fast passing away, they will not relax their hitherto ceaseless efforts to have the crime brought home to the villain who committed it.

Mr Powys-Keck continued to live at The Knoll until his death in about 1912; by that time he was a JP and a Deputy Lord-Lieutenant.

A plaque was unveiled to the memory of PC Frederick Atkins in New Malden High Street in 1996.

CHAPTER 9

The Major and his Wayward Son 1888

You had better speak to me: it is a matter of life or death.

Middle-class murders are unusual in real life, though not in the pages of fiction. This was an exception to the rule and, in a year overshadowed by the deeds of a more infamous (and anonymous) criminal, it has been all but forgotten. The autumn of 1888 had been, in any case, a grim one in the locality of Kingston. There had been a railway accident at Hampton Wick, where four people had been burnt to death; a drayman was killed in Thames Street, Kingston, and a man was killed in the hayfield near the town. Then there were two deaths by gunshots which are about to be detailed.

Thomas Hare, born in Ireland in 1817, joined the 27th Regiment, the Royal Inniskillings Fusiliers, on 27 March 1835, as an ensign. He became a lieutenant on 11 November 1838. He switched to a colonial unit, becoming a captain on 1 April 1847 in the Cape Mounted Rifles in South Africa and saw distinguished service in the Kaffir Wars, reaching the rank of major on 26 October 1858 and being awarded the Kaffir Medal. He should, after his retirement shortly afterwards, have had a pleasing life. He had married Frances (born in 1828) from Cape Town and they had at least five sons: Gordon Horace (the third oldest), born in 1855, Waltham, born in 1861 and lastly Maynard, born in 1867. The latter two went into business, as City clerks. After residing in Bournemouth and then Harrow, in the 1860s, since about 1876, they had lived in St James' Road, Kingston, a street lived in by the middle class. Dr Holberton, who had examined the corpse of Sarah Martin in 1872, lived there.

Hare lived a fairly retired life, not taking a prominent part in local affairs, as a magistrate or a councillor, as some retired officers did. Yet his local friends talked of his kindness. He was also a keen churchgoer, though he did not attend any one particular church. He also attended meetings of the Liberal Party, supporting local candidates. He was a very healthy man and thought nothing of regularly walking long distances.

Yet there was a fly in the ointment. Gordon Hare was that fly. It is not certain exactly what the reason for his falling out with his father was, but it concerned money. Although his brothers settled down into the ordered world of work, he did not. Perhaps he could not. In 1873, he went to America to pursue cattle farming. He spent most of his adult life abroad, including spells in Australia and Mexico, and had a gift for languages, being able to speak four or five. At first his parents had indulged him to the extent of giving him several thousand pounds. His ventures abroad had not been a success. The money spent, he returned from America to England in 1885, but he was not a prodigal son. He began to threaten his father, to such a serious extent that his father took the extreme step of charging him before the magistrates. Certainly the old man went in fear of his life.

At the magistrates' court, in November 1885, the major told the sorry story. As soon as Gordon returned, he had called on his parents and demanded money from them. They told him that he had no claim on them. He returned and caused a scene. He threatened to shoot his father, but he claimed that if his father could not find him a job, he would have to go to the workhouse or kill his father and then commit suicide. Given that he had resisted arrest and had a revolver on his person, his father's testimony was enough for him to be found guilty of threatening words. He was told by the magistrates that he must find sureties for his good behaviour or be gaoled for three months. Lacking any money, he was imprisoned for the time mentioned.

On leaving gaol in the following year, he is alleged to have openly repeated his threats. In February 1887, Hare thought about bringing charges again, but was talked out of it. Gordon then went abroad.

Gordon returned to England in August 1888 and took up residence in Burlington Road, Bayswater. On Friday 24 August, he was seen by Maynard, who lived with his parents, when the latter was leaving his offices. Maynard tried to avoid him, but was unsuccessful, and told Gordon, 'It is no use for me to speak to you, everybody has tried to speak to you, but it is no good.' His brother replied, 'You had better speak to me: it is a matter of life or death.' The two brothers then lunched together. Maynard was shown some revolver cartridges and his elder brother talked about his money troubles and how no one would help him. There was no explicit threat made against anyone, least of all their father. Gordon then visited his parents, a fact he mentioned to his brother. The major spoke quietly, but firmly to his wayward son, telling him that if he did not leave, he would be trespassing. Martha Hodsell, a housemaid, was instructed not to admit Gordon should he call again.

It should be noted that Major Hare was not in a position to do much more to financially help his wayward son. On his death, he had but £41 2s 6d. There were no Army pensions for those leaving the forces until 1872; instead, officers sold the commissions they had first paid for, often investing the cash in order to provide an income.

On the following day, Gordon visited his brother's place of business. He showed him a number of revolver cartridges and talked of 'a matter of life and death', but did not directly threaten their father. Maynard knew that his brother was excitable, especially on the subject of money and he was convinced that he had been ill treated financially and should receive all the help he needed. It should be noted that he was given one guinea a week by his parents which would be enough to prevent him starving. He told Maynard that he was taking sleeping draughts in large quantities. Gordon spent the Saturday night in a hotel in Kingston.

The climax came on the Sunday evening of 26 August 1888. Major Hare had attended St Mark's church that evening, as he usually did. Whilst he was at prayer, Gordon called at the family house, at about 7.10 pm but when the housemaid saw who it was, she did not open the door. After waiting on the steps for a

St Mark's church, Surbiton, 1900s. Author's collection

few minutes, he tried the back door and then went away, but not for long, for he was waiting for when his father, when he finished his walk home and was on the threshold, unaware of who was waiting for him. It was just before 8 pm.

It is uncertain whether the Major saw his son or spoke even briefly to him. It was a busy road and he was not expecting to see him there. But as soon as he had opened the gate to the house and had rang the door bell, Gordon addressed him in an angry tone, then pulled out a revolver and discharged two bullets into his father, who fell at once. Then a third shot was fired and the killer dropped to the ground, too. Mrs Hare opened the door on hearing the shots and subsequently fainted at the sight. This was no surprise. Her husband was lying over the gate and her son lay on the steps, but was still breathing. Dr Matthew Owen Coleman was also on hand at once – he had indeed attended the same church service as the major, but left after he had. He examined the body of the major, but he was already dead. On his recommendation, Gordon was sent to Surbiton Cottage Hospital, which was on the other side of the road, but despite being given brandy, he died a few minutes after admission. The police were called, with Inspector Thornby and PC Butcher being quickly on hand.

The murder weapon was obvious. It was the six- chambered revolver which Gordon still clutched in his right hand. He had shot his father in the neck, severing the blood vessels there. He had then put the barrel of the gun into his own mouth and pulled the trigger. The bullet had entered his brain and killed him shortly afterwards. Thornby searched the body. He found spare cartridges, a little money and a letter from a man in the tea business, informing Gordon that he could not recommend him for employment. The gun was confiscated by PC Alfred Mitchener.

Dr Braxton Hicks was the coroner who oversaw the inquest at the Cottage Hospital on 28 August. The jury had the nauseous task of trooping into the major's study where his body lay, then returned to the hospital to see the son's body, which was in a coffin in the hospital mortuary. The policemen, doctor and Maynard Hare all gave evidence. The conclusion was that this was murder followed by suicide. Dr Hicks suggested that the only ray of comfort from the whole tragedy was that the family had been spared the ordeal of a murder trial which could only have resulted in Gordon's being hanged. A message of sympathy was sent to the grieving widow. On the same day, the major and his son were buried in the same grave in Kingston Cemetery. His widow soon left the house and went to live in Parklands, Surbiton Hill, dying there in 1893.

This was a shocking crime. Although we don't know the full details of the story leading up to the double shooting, it does seem that Gordon had wasted the money his parents had given him, but could not accept that they could not give him any more large sums. Perhaps his father's sympathy was less than it should have been, but to threaten to kill him was a step too far. To murder his own father was the ultimate revenge on the man who he thought had wronged him.

Ironically, in London's East End, on the day after the inquest, Polly Nichols was killed and mutilated by an unknown man subsequently known as Jack the Ripper – she was perhaps his first victim – and poor Major Hare was forgotten by the newspaper reading public.

Chapter 10

The First Fred West 1894

Barnes Common is a rather lonely spot, and does not bear the best of reputations.

Exactly a century before grim revelations were made at Cromwell Road, Gloucester, one Fred West was at the centre of another murder investigation. Although his predecessor was almost certainly unknown to the multiple murderer of the early 1990s, it is an eerie coincidence. Although this case was not as terrible as the later one, it did leave the police and public with unfinished business on their hands, whereas at least the later case was cleared up.

James Robert Wells was born in Somers Town, London, in 1863. In 1891, he was living with his widowed stepmother and one of his sisters (both named Maria), in a house in Glenthorne Road, Hammersmith; indeed he had lived in Hammersmith for most of his life. His occupation was that of

Glenthorne Road, 2009. The Author

a butcher and he lived above the shop. Although he was a teetotaller, he enjoyed gambling and this may have led him to his untimely demise in 1894. He was also a bachelor.

On Thursday evening, 1 May 1894, Wells had been at his younger brother's house on Tabor Road, Hammersmith. Josiah Richard Wells later recalled that his brother left the house at about 10.45 pm, and was walking his sisters home safely to their home in Winchmore Street, Putney. Miss Alice Ada and Miss Jane Wells thus accompanied their brother. He did not plan to walk the entire way with them, but would see them past the lonely stretch on Barnes Common. He left them at the Lodge, near Rock Lane on the west side of the common. The time was about 11.20 pm. Ada saw him begin his return trip and that was the last time she saw him alive. What happened next is unclear, but what is certain is that Wells was attacked.

Perhaps we should pause for a moment to consider a contemporary assessment of the Common on which the tragedy was about to occur:

> Barnes Common is a rather lonely spot, and does not bear the best of reputations. The roads converge near the spot where the body was found, but the nearest house is that of the Common keeper. The common is a pleasant enough place during the day time, and just now is in the fresh green of early spring time. Many who live in Hammersmith enjoy a walk amongst the gorse and undergrowth, but at night time most respectable people avoid the spot for the simple reason that it is then the resort of loose characters of both sexes. It would not be at all surprising for anyone to be stopped and robbed there, although murder is a length to which the footpad does not usually go.

The attack cannot have happened much after his sisters last saw him, because just after 11.30 pm, William Robertson Patterson, a merchant of Putney Common, was on the scene. Patterson had taken a cab from Hammersmith Bridge, to his home, but had decided to alight before he arrived there, because he thought it would be a quicker journey if he cut across the footpath rather than taking the cab on the longer way round on the road. He walked along the footpath to

Barnes Common, c1900. Author's collection

Rock's Lane and then heard cries for help. This was from a place only 130 yards from where the common keeper's cottage was located and 200 yards from Crofts Lane. It was here where he found the dying Wells. Wells was probably taken by surprise because he was a tall and muscular man, as one would imagine a butcher would need to be, and he had a stick with him. He may well have been surprised, because of the dark night, visibility was at a premium. Patterson asked the man to get up, but he could not do so, nor could he speak. He was, however, still breathing. He then thought he saw something or someone moving in the direction of Putney, but he could not be sure whether he had or not, 'because it would be difficult to tell a man from a tree at that distance'.

Patterson then tried to find anyone he could. These turned out to be two cyclists, Samuel Letts of Shepherd's Bush and Joseph Marshall of Paddington. They went over to where the body lay. Patterson saw a man crossing the footbridge nearby, on his way to Putney. This was Henry Stallman, a commercial traveller, of Putney, who, on being told of the injured man, went with one of the cyclists to fetch the common keeper at about 11.40 pm. This was Henry Sergent, who had just turned

Barnes railway station, 2009. The Author

in after returning from patrolling the common at 11.15; he had then been from the *Red Lion* to Putney Common and back and had seen nothing untoward. He quickly dressed and joined the other three – Stallman then departed.

The four men looked at the body of a man lying on the ground, a few yards from the path. His coat had been shuffled up his back as if he had been dragged by his feet. Then they washed the man's face, which was bloodstained. Sergent blew his whistle to alert any policemen in the vicinity. This was heard at 11.50 pm by PS Alfred Cole, who was on Queen's Road, Barnes, and who ran to the scene, where he found the four men standing near the dying man. Other constables arrived shortly afterwards. James Eyre, on duty at Barnes railway station, also heard the whistle and came along to investigate.

In the meantime, finding that the man was not dead, PS Cole asked him a number of questions, the dialogue as follows:

'What is your name?'
'Wells.'
'Where do you live?'
'21 Glenthorne Road, Hammersmith.'
'Who did this?'
'West, West.'
'Who?'
'Fred West.'
'Where does he live?'
'21 Glenthorne Road. I came across the Common and he did it.'
'Did he strike you unawares?'
'Yes.'
'Had you anything to drink?'
'No.'
'Been to the *Red Lion*?'
'No.'
'*Boileau*?'

This was presumably a reference to the nearby *Boileau Arms*. Wells' final words were, 'I am cold, lift me up.'

At 11.45, at Bridge Road, Barnes, Acting PS Hunt met a man who told him that a murder had been committed on the Common. It would have taken about fifteen minutes to have walked from the place of the crime to where the sergeant was. This man may have been Stallman.

There were a few clues lying nearby. One was undoubtedly the murder weapon. It was a piece of iron, perhaps once part of a cart wheel, which had been flattened out. There were bloodstains on it and on a nearby handkerchief, probably used by the killer to wipe the weapon clean of blood. There was also a hat and a walking stick nearby, but the latter was clean.

In Well's pockets were 30s in silver, four pence in bronze coins, a steel watch chain and a new silver watch, a ruled race card and the rules of the Cork Club. Amongst the papers found was a memorandum in which West was named and the letters 'pd' were stated. On another paper, the same name appeared, with the letters 'np' against it. It was surmised that these referred to money that Wells owed West for gambling successes and that 'pd' meant paid and that 'np' meant not paid. The writing on these notes was identified as being that of Wells.

Two doctors examined the dying man. Dr Frederick Welstead, of White Lodge, Lower Richmond Road, appears to have been the first, summoned shortly after midnight by the police. He found Wells semi-conscious. The face was washed and there was no brain matter protruding. There were scalp wounds on the back of the neck. There was also a wound on the forehead, probably caused when the victim was lying on the ground. Some of the victim's teeth had been knocked out.

Wells was then taken to the West London Hospital, where the house surgeon, Robert Ross Setter, examined him. His clothes were covered in blood and he was evidently dying. Additional wounds were found on the man's right forehand and on the back of his right hand, where he had probably raised his arm to try and defend himself. During the autopsy, he concluded that there were about forty separate wounds to the head, which had resulted in multiple fractures to the skull, any one of which would have caused death. All this suggested that this had been a ferocious attack, caused by far more savagery and force than would be necessary to ensure that Wells would die. John Wells, younger brother to the deceased, identified his late brother in the early hours of that day.

With the dying words of the deceased in mind, Inspector Pugsley and Detective Sergeant Hawkins went to Glenthorne Road on 7.40 am on the morning after the murder. They saw West at the corner of Cambridge Road. He was described as 'a rather short man, with bronzed face and iron-grey moustache'. West had been born in Hayes, Middlesex in 1837, but now lived with his family in York Road, Hammersmith and was employed as a wood sawyer at Kirkman's piano factory. He was known by all as 'a quiet and inoffensive fellow'. Pugsley walked over to him and said, 'Your name is Frederick West?'

'No, my name is Alfred West,' was the reply.

Pugsley explained who he was and that West was acquainted with Wells, who had been murdered on the Common on the previous night. Furthermore, he was going to arrest him on suspicion because the dying man had identified him as his assailant. West objected, saying, 'If he is dead, how could he say that I did it?'

Pugsley explained and then cautioned his prisoner. West trembled. On their way to Hammersmith Police Station, West said, 'I am surprised. I saw him last night about seven, and bought some sausages from him.' He was later formally charged at Barnes police station. He said, 'I have not been to Barnes for some months until this morning. Three or four weeks ago I was at the *Boïleau Arms* for a glass of beer.'

The murder created great local excitement. People flocked to the Common to see the scene of the crime. They also gawped outside Wells' home in Glenthorne Road. And they clamoured to attend the inquest. The local press in Richmond and Hammersmith also catered to this demand for murder news.

The inquest was begun at the Hammersmith Coroner's Court on 6 May. Wells' sisters gave evidence of when they last saw him. A description of the discovery of the corpse and Wells' last words were then given, followed by the medical details, all of which has already been related.

There was speculation as to why Wells had been killed. One theory was that robbery was the motive, but if so it was odd that none of Wells' money had been taken, though as against that, it was possible that the thief had been disturbed by the arrival of Stallman. Another possibility was that someone had personal reasons for hating Wells – perhaps this was a crime of passion or revenge for a past wrong or the result from a more recent quarrel. Yet everyone spoke of Wells as being a quiet and harmless individual who had apparently not an enemy in the world.

Gambling might have provided a reason. As well as being a butcher, Wells was a bookmaker and took bets on horses. One of his clients was West. Could there have been a quarrel over unpaid gambling debts? Yet everyone stated that the two men were on good terms, and in any case, the amounts involved seemed too small for any murderous attack.

Josiah Wells, a brother to the deceased, stated that the common could be a dangerous place and recounted an experience of his there:

> I was stopped myself, a short time ago, while taking my sisters home to Putney, by a man who sprang out of the dark and flourished a stick, but disappeared when he saw I was not alone.

Setter was asked whether a man in the condition that Wells was in would have been able to have given intelligible answers, and he thought perhaps not. The coroner summed up, concluding Wells' last words could not be taken as being accurate and that the debt of 2s 2d was hardly an amount to have led to murder. Therefore, there was no one whom suspicion pointed. He adjourned the inquest for a week.

On the following day Wells was buried. There were crowds of people along the route from Glenthorne Road to St John's church, where the service was conducted by two clergymen. Five mourning coaches followed the open car, where the coffin was loaded down with wreaths. Apart from family members, local tradesmen also turned out en masse to pay their respects at church and cemetery.

The inquest was concluded on Thursday 11 May. The matter attracted much public attention, for both the court and its precincts were packed with spectators. West had to be conveyed there in a cab. He was placed on the witness bench and at first appeared flushed and nervous, as well he might, before relaxing and becoming merely passively interested.

No evidence could be brought against West. In fact, several witnesses spoke on his behalf. Pugsley stated that his clothes and house had been examined, but there were no traces of blood and nothing suspicious whatsoever. Apart from the man's betting, there was nothing known against his character. No motive apart from the gambling debt of 2s 2d could be found.

Alfred John Bailey, West's foreman, spoke up on his man's behalf. He had seen him at the *Royal Oak* on Glethorne Road at 8.10 pm on the night of the murder. They had remained there until 9.40 pm and then went to West's home, where he saw him indoors. He added that there was nothing like the weapon used which could be found at the works. Florence West, West's daughter, recalled the two men coming to the door at about 9.40 pm. West then went to bed, after some conversation. Florence and her sister Ada were downstairs that night until past midnight, preparing things for their mother, also called Ada, who was aged forty-three, and was unwell. The younger Ada bolted the front door at 11 pm. Early next morning, Florence told her father to stop snoring or he would awake her mother. Ada recalled seeing her father at 11 pm, when he told her to keep a good fire in his wife's bedroom. He woke next morning at 6.30 am as usual. William Butler, a lodger, remembered coming home that night and seeing West at 10.10 pm at the house. Thomas Clarke, manager at the factory where West worked, said West had worked there for a number of years and bore an excellent character.

After some consultation with his solicitor, West made a statement before the court:

> I left off work at 7 o'clock on Tuesday 1st May. I went on to Cambridge Road and in the Glenthorne Road I called at Wells' shop. I bought a pound of sausages from him. I was there most nights of the week. I went on shopping further so as to keep the children at home attending to their mother. After the shopping I went to the *Royal Oak*. I stayed there from shortly after eight to twenty minutes to ten, and Alfred Bailey and I walked home together. We stopped at the door until my daughter came to open it: then I bade him goodnight and he went away. I went into the kitchen and gave the goods to my daughter. I went upstairs afterwards to my wife, while one of my daughters came down to get supper, and went to bed. I was called at half past six the next morning to have breakfast and I went out to work at 7.30.

There then followed some discussion about the serious nature of the case, and that everything had been done to shed light on it, albeit unsuccessfully. The coroner said that the Common was desolate and tree lined, and that it would be easy to attack someone there and then to escape. The police did not think the open space was particularly dangerous, though rough sleepers were often found there. Assaults there were rare. The coroner thought that the motive could have been revenge or it could have been robbery, though he thought both were unlikely, and that there was no corroboration of the deceased's statement that West was responsible. The inquest was concluded on this unsatisfactory, because inconclusive, note, and West was congratulated by his colleagues for being made a free man once more. It is assumed that that none of West's family were lying to protect him.

West was very relieved to be out of custody. He had spent over a week at Holloway prison and the experience had not agreed with him. The food and bedding was poor. There was daily exercise in the yard, daily chapel services and books to read – he had enjoyed reading a history of the Fire Brigade. Because his wife was ill, he had had a friend write letters to her purporting to be from him, saying that he was away on business. Pugsley apologised for detaining him. West had no idea why Wells mentioned his name and stated, 'I had known him for years. We had little transactions together, but apart from that we were fond of one another's company. We often met, and enjoyed a chat, both on week days and Sundays. Wells was always cheerful and good natured.'

A reader of the *West London Observer*, 'Justitia', speculated about the murder in print. He thought that the handkerchief which the murder weapon had been wrapped in, was an overlooked but significant clue. He thought that the killer's name or some other marking on it might give the identity of the murderer away. He thought that the attack was motivated by revenge or passion and that the victim's past should be examined. Or the killer might be 'a dangerous lunatic'. Should such be the case, the sooner he is found the better; otherwise the late murder may be supplemented by others, just as in the case of the notorious "Ripper" crimes which made such a sensation some years ago. In any case, Barnes Common should be under police supervision for some time to come'.

Most cases of unsolved murder result in someone coming forward to confess to the crime; almost always a man who has absolutely no connection with the matter. This one was no exception. Shortly after the inquest proceedings had closed, a young man went to Hammersmith Police Station early one evening on 17 May. He gave his name as Frederick Albert Welch, a twenty-five-year-old builder and bookmaker. He handed a written confession to Inspector Harry Ashwell. The police officer was told that the young man killed Wells because the latter owed him £120 in gambling debts. He was sent to Barnes police station, where Pugsley read through the confession to the man and entered his details on the charge sheet. When being asked if he had anything to say after the charge had been read out, he said that the address he had written in the confession was wrong and that he refused to tell them the real one. He added, about the charge, 'I object to the "malice aforethought", that is quite a different thing. I had no intention of killing at the time.'

On the following day, the man was brought before the Richmond magistrates, where he was charged. He was remanded in custody on the strength of his confession. However, enquiries revealed that his real name was Frederick Albert Davies, of Argoed House, Castleneau, Barnes. He had once been apprenticed on the sailing ship, Enterkin, where, in 1889, he had fallen down the hold and had injured his head. So seriously were his wounds that his mental health had been adversely affected thereafter.

Davies, to give the man his correct name, reappeared before the magistrates on 22 May. He handed them a letter. In it, he stated that his confession was 'a lie from beginning to end'. In order to avoid wasting any more time, he added that he was a married man, and was not a bookmaker and knew no more about the crime than what he had read in the newspapers. His letter concluded, 'Why I should have put together such a fabrication of abominable lies I cannot tell. I believe it to be temporary insanity'. Pugsley had in the meantime been making additional enquiries and found that Davies was not guilty. He was thus released.

This brought the case back to square one. Who had killed Wells, and why? Robbery is a possibility, but if so, why did the attacker add murder to theft by striking far more than was necessary? If the murder was intended and was by someone known to Wells, who either followed him or had arranged to meet him on the common, it seems odd that no one knew who could be responsible – after all, Wells had lived in the locality for all his adult life. One assumes that none of the men known to be on the common that night – Stallman and Patterson – had anything to do with the crime. It seems unlikely that if they had that they would not have left the scene as quickly as possible. The other question is why did Wells mention West as he lay dying? Perhaps it was delirium, for Alfred West seems to have been at home at the time of the murder, according to his and his family's testimonies. Could Wells have been mistaken for someone else in the dark? This, perhaps, is the most likely explanation, but it only leaves further questions; namely, who was the intended victim, and were they killed at a later date?

CHAPTER 11

A Suicide Pact 1905

I am going to take this; it will end it once and for ever.

Most well known cases of poisoning are among the middle classes, such as the Crippens, the Maybricks and the case detailed in this book (chapter 3). However, in reality, poisoning is more common among the poor and the desperate, although these are usually little known. This case is one of them.

John and Marion Seddon, who had been married in about 1893, ran a small confectioner's shop in Mortlake High Street from June 1905, having recently moved there from Staines, where they had run a similar business. It did not prosper. In fact, takings were only a few shillings a day. This meant that they were going to have trouble paying their annual rent of £36, which was due in October. John's health was poor, and he was seventy-eight years old (his wife was fifty-five). He rarely went out in the day time, but took short walks in the evenings. Dr Charles Batchelor, of Staines, had been attending them professionally since 1898. Seddon had been suffering from diabetes and his wife once had neuralgia. In 1901, he prescribed liniment and some mixture and in 1904 there was a repeat prescription, which included an ounce of belladonna. She had six bottles of this. Relations between the two were problematic, with Seddon being increasingly quarrelsome – though usually he was easy going – and even having had a knife taken out of his hand on two occasions.

In September, Marion Harms, of Walthamstow, who was Mrs Seddon's niece, came to stay with them. She realised her relatives were in a difficult situation and were worrying about money. On 11 September, Mrs Seddon asked her to write to Elizabeth Barrett, whose late husband was Mrs Seddon's

Mortlake High Road, 2009. The Author

brother, asking for help with the furniture. The Seddons were planning to leave before quarter day because of their inability to pay the rent. On that night, Marion slept in the same bedroom as Mrs Barrett, which was on the first floor. The Seddons slept in the back room on the same floor.

On the following morning, at 8am, Marion recalled that Mrs Seddon entered and said something about 30s. Apparently, 'she was in her night dress and looked rather unsteady – as she went out of the room she staggered when she got to the door'. Marion then went downstairs and made some tea, taking it up to Mrs Seddon. However, her aunt waved her away. She then decided to call Dr Robert Mackintosh. It was now about 8.20am and in another twenty-five minutes, he arrived. He recalled, 'I found them in bed together – he was in a comatose state, suffering from collapse, and I diagnosed he was suffering from belladonna [extracted from the deadly nightshade plant] poisoning.' His wife was in a similar condition.

Mackintosh attended them for two hours, administering antidotes and using a stomach pump. After he had used every method he could think of, and after two hours, Mrs Seddon seemed to be improving, but the same could not be said of her husband, who was visibly weaker. He had the pair sent to hospital and called the police. He also looked about the room and recalled, 'I saw this bottle on the table on the left hand side of the bed, empty, it was quite dry inside – I also saw a tumbler, there, which was dry – they both smell of belladonna liniment – I estimated that the poison had been taken about two hours before I went there – I judged her husband had taken the larger dose'.

The two poison victims were then sent to the Royal Hospital at Richmond. Dr William Davidson was house surgeon on their arrival, so he dealt with them. They arrived that afternoon and Davidson stated:

> The deceased was in a deeply comatose state, his face pale, and his breathing was very shallow – he was unconscious and remained so for some hours, when he became delirious and started vomiting – those are symptoms of belladonna poisoning – he remained in that state until 6.30 pm the next day, when he died.

A post-mortem held on the following day confirmed the doctor's diagnosis. By 14 September, Marion was recovering and the doctor asked her what had happened. She said that at 6.30 am that morning, she had taken the bottle of liniment and had divided it into two unequal parts. They had then both drunk it and had taken an ounce of belladonna between them.

There was an inquest on 21 September, when Marion had recovered sufficiently to be present. She was examined, but not cross-examined and made the following statement:

> I have only to say that my husband has been in a miserable depressed condition for a long time; for the last two years

> our circumstances have been getting desperate, and we decided that as there was no means of earning a living, we had better leave the world together. On this morning in particular I had been laying wake and worrying; then I jumped out of bed and I said, 'I can stand this wear and tear no longer; I'll end it.' I took the bottle and the glass and poured out the biggest part of the poison. I said, 'I am going to take this; it will end it once and for ever.' He just said, 'You won't.' I said, 'I will,' and I drank it off. Then I said, 'I have left enough for you; will you have it?' I said, 'It means this or the workhouse.' He said, 'Yes give it to me.' I poured it out and he snatched it out of my hand. I put the bottle back and got into bed.

She then went upstairs and told Mrs Barrett what they had just done, and that there was 30s in the house which she should use to get them buried cheaply and quietly. She also told her to take Miss Harms home safely, then, feeling a pain in her chest, left the bedroom and returned to her husband, and recalled:

> My husband was lying just where I had left him, on the edge of the bedstead. He opened his eyes and looked, so I just said, 'I have just been and wakened Lizzie and told her what we have done.' He said, 'Come and get into bed then.' They were the last words he spoke. I remember nothing more … I took the biggest portion, as I thought it would take more to kill me.

Another piece of evidence which was brought forward was a letter that her late husband had written to her, and had put in his pocket. It read:

> My last request and Desire is that you should dispose of all our effects and live on the results as long as it lasts and then follow me as your case is now hopeless. Above all pray Don't be ruled by your Demon Mother. Instead of which you by order of your mother are giving all your own goods away and are saving your neither so that she may bring her Beauty out

> and plank on you and claim all as hers and make you her Slave. This is all arranged. What a Blind Fool you must be not to see through it and won't listen to anyone else. To my Wife.

The 'Demon Mother' was Sarah Barrett, born in Essex in 1822 and whom the Seddons had lived with when in Clarence Street, Staines. Clearly Seddon believed she had a malign influence over his wife.

The verdict of the jury was that Seddon had died from exhaustion following the effects of belladonna and aconite, taking his own life whilst in a state of temporary insanity due to money troubles. DS Golden Barrell then arrested her for the murder of her husband by aiding him in taking poison. She was taken to the police station to have the charge read to her, to which she did not reply. Seven days later she appeared before the Mortlake magistrates' court and was committed for trial, spending the next few weeks in Holloway.

The case came before the Old Bailey on 16 October and the charge was one of murder (to assist another with suicide was treated as a capital offence). After all the evidence and witnesses had been brought before the jury, the inevitable verdict was given – guilty. However, the foreman of the jury said, 'We wish her to be strongly recommended to mercy; we are unanimous on that point.' And indeed, that was what happened. Marion Seddon was not hanged. Mrs Seddon had told the court, 'I did not kill my husband.'

So ended a most dismal and tragic case, where two people decided that the only way out of their money problems was to commit suicide. However, a reprieve was granted and the death sentence was commuted to one of imprisonment.

CHAPTER 12

An Accountant's Deadly Reckoning 1927

I can find no solution in all my problems here, so I am going to look for one on the other side.

Alexander Bell Filson had come a long way since his humble beginnings in Portaferry, County Down, in 1877. By 1906 he began to work for Maurice Chater, a City accountant, as a clerk, in his offices in Cheapside, at Chater and Egerton. On 12 January 1907, he married Bessie Eliza Head (born in Mortlake in 1883) and in the following years, three children were born: John Warnock (10 June 1908), Maragret Warnock (14 December 1912) and Mary Warnock (7 November 1917). They were living in Coulter Road, Hammersmith in 1911. The two girls attended Putney High School and in 1927 John was a bank clerk. In 1912, Filson became an associate of the Institute of Chartered Accountants. During the war, Filson was rewarded for his financial acumen by Chater and was made a partner, earning about £1,200 per annum – about ten times that of the average working man (equal to c.£68,500 today). Chater and Egerton was dissolved in 1920, to be replaced by Chater and Filson. Chater was on visiting terms with the Filsons and knew his wife. He thought that Filson was devoted to his wife and children. In 1924, the Filsons moved to River View Gardens, Barnes, overlooking the Thames.

However, matters began to go wrong in the following years. On 11 October 1925, his wife died from cancer, which had been a long drawn out process. Filson told Mrs Woollard before his wife's death, 'You know your sister's going, and if it were not for the children, I would go with her.' Yet he later

Cheapside, 1900s. Author's collection

promised not to kill himself. Even so, this had a great effect on him and his career. In the following year, Filson had taken his holiday in September. It was then that Chater realised something was wrong. There were 'irregularities' which was presumably another way of saying that Filson had been embezzling money, to the tune of £371. The partnership was dissolved and on 30 September, Filson was out of a job. His only comment to his former partner was that he must have been mad. The motive was probably that Filson was spending heavily and needed money desperately. A note read at the inquest said that Filson had borrowed £484 from Chater at 6% interest. Filson was briefly in business on his own, with offices in Philpott Lane, but it did not last long.

Life seemed to go on. Miss Ruth Parrish, from Stockton-on-Tees, who had been the live-in housekeeper since November 1926, recalled that her employer was speaking 'in a queer manner' on Monday 9 January 1927. He was worrying about the untidiness of his daughters who threw things about the house. But later that day, he seemed unconcerned about it and laughed it off.

Riverview Gardens, 2009.
The Author

On Thursday 13 January, Filson's only brother, James, a deputy inspector general in the Indian Police, was on leave, staying at the *Regent Palace Hotel*, and rang up his brother. He wanted to see him, and Filson arranged that his brother and sister in law would come over for Sunday lunch. The two had not met since November 1926.

Events were moving rapidly by the following day. Filson returned home at 6 pm and seemed quite normal. At dinner he was even jolly. Margaret, who had been ill for a few days, ate in her dressing gown, before going to bed at 8.45 pm. Oddly enough, for the past few days (since 11 January), Filson had been sleeping in the same room as Margaret; usually he and his son shared a bedroom and the two girls slept in the other. At 9 pm that night, Miss Parrish went to her room, to write a letter. Just before she did so, Filson told her, for the first time, about the impending visit of his brother and his wife. She turned in at 10.10 pm.

However, she could not sleep because the light in the hall was kept on and it shone into her room through a glass panel in the top of the door. Until midnight she heard subdued voices coming from the drawing room, but she could not hear who was talking. Then silence reigned. The light in the hall was finally expunged at 2.10am. Ten minutes later she heard a strange noise, as if a piece of metal had been put through a pane of glass. Then the sound was repeated. Miss Parrish paid no attention to these noises, because, living by the river as they did, she was used to hearing odd sounds at night. The last sound of the night was as if a spanner was being dropped on the asphalt outside. After that she fell asleep, not waking until the alarm clock went off at a quarter to seven.

She then rose, put the kettle on and made tea, which she took up to the two bedrooms, but on knocking at both, received no answer, though this was not unusual, as she explained, 'the children had been keeping late hours at parties during the holidays and were in the custom of getting up late'. At 9.30am, a friend of John's visited him. On that day John was due to go to Lincoln to join the RAF, and the friend was calling to say goodbye. Mr Filson had earlier said that he would be sad to see him go, but did not want to stand in his son's way, 'I shall miss Jack very much, but the boy seems keen on it.' He was not depressed about it and had said that the discipline would do him good. She told John's friend that John was not out of bed yet. But Miss Parrish had seen a number of objects on the table in the dining room and was worried by them. They included two envelopes, but more alarming, in an open drawer nearby was a document headed 'Cemetery. East Sheen'. Most worrying of all was a box of revolver cartridges on the table. Fighting back panic, she immediately went upstairs and knocked on John's room. There was no reply, so she went inside and saw the lad lying on his back near the door. Although the blind was down, she could see he was dead. Turning on the light, she saw Mary's corpse, too. She later recalled:

> There was blood also on her, and I could see that she was dead. Both the bodies were covered with the bed clothes. It was a great shock to me. I stood for a moment just where I was, and then went out and shut the door. There was a girl servant there and I did not want her to see what had happened.

Thinking that she would see similar sights in the room next door, she went to fetch the police. On her return, she told the maid, 'They are all dead. Please go home.' When Detective Inspector Cooper arrived, she accompanied him to the room. They found Filson lying across the bed, and Mary was nearby. All corpses were dressed in nightwear, and Filson was wearing a dressing gown. The glass on a photograph on the wall had been smashed, too. Miss Parrish was particularly shocked because she had never seen him in a morbid state about his wife's death and thought he was devoting his life to his children. Furthermore, she never knew that her late employer had a revolver in his possession, but then she had only worked in the house for two months. Filson evidently had kept it secret.

Dr James Scott, of Upper Richmond Road, Putney, conducted the post-mortem. All four had died from a single revolver wound to the head. Additionally, Mary had two wounds on her right cheek where a bullet had entered and departed. It had been the shock following the shooting that had killed the four people. The gun used was a small calibre .25 Browning automatic pistol. All the shootings had occurred within a very short space of time.

The other important pieces of evidence were in the letters. Both were from Filson. The first was addressed to his brother and it read as follows:

> My Dear Jim – My head won't stand any more of the hell I have been living in for the past two years. It breaks my heart to see Bessie's home going to rack and ruin. The girls are almost neglected when I am not here. I do not know what to do for them. If Bessie could only have stayed with me it would have all been so different. This will release Jack and Peggy's share of the trust. Goodbye, old man. Better luck to you – Alec.

The second note was to his former partner:

> Dear Chater – I can find no solution in all my problems here, so I am going to look for one on the other side. Perhaps this will make things easier for you in certain quarters, some of which you are not aware of. Yours, A. Filson.
>
> P.S. Try and be a little more human in future. You have a lot to learn in the ways of humanity still. The narrow way is not for all in this world.

Chater told the police, 'He never threatened to take his life in my hearing … He was devotedly attached to his wife and children.' He recalled asking Filson, 'I suppose you have constantly lived beyond your means', to which his former partner had replied, 'I don't think so, although I have been rather near the mark up to the time of the wife's illness, which, of course, entailed a great number of extra expenses.'

The inquest was held at Mortlake on Wednesday 19 January. James Filson identified his brother's body. He also stated that having gone through his papers, he realised that Filson's financial affairs were at a low ebb. After the witnesses gave evidence, the coroner warned the jury that the evidence, apart from that contained in the letters, did not lead to the inevitable conclusion that Filson had killed his three children and then himself. However, the jury quickly concluded that Filson, whilst his mind was unbalanced, had shot his three children dead in the early hours of Saturday 15 January, then ended his own life.

Filson was a reserved, moody man. The police concluded, 'From a search of his papers, and enquiries which we made, it is fairly evident that the tragedy was wholly due to his financial troubles.' Yet it is worth noting that on death he had £1,010 5s 11d, which went to his brother.

Why he killed himself is not entirely clear, but his money worries and the death of his wife were preying on his mind and leading him to believe that he was unable to give his children the life they should have. Perhaps the imminent meeting with his more successful brother and the equally imminent departure of his son were the final straws to spur him into action. In order to successfully end it all for his family, he knew he would have to act now. He did so, and with appalling results.

CHAPTER 13

Murder in the Park (1) 1927

You are the last person she was supposed to meet and its funny she hasn't been home.

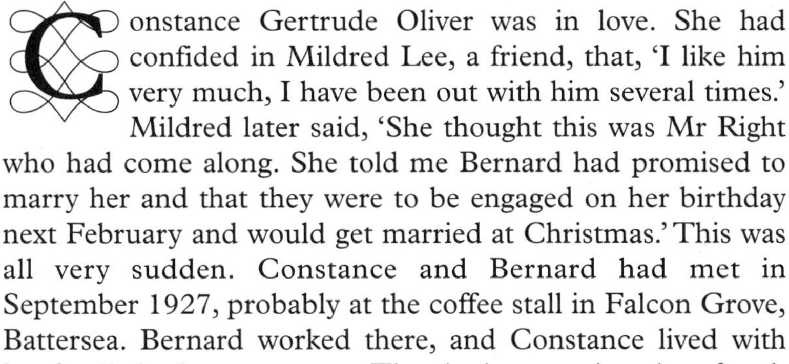

Constance Gertrude Oliver was in love. She had confided in Mildred Lee, a friend, that, 'I like him very much, I have been out with him several times.' Mildred later said, 'She thought this was Mr Right who had come along. She told me Bernard had promised to marry her and that they were to be engaged on her birthday next February and would get married at Christmas.' This was all very sudden. Constance and Bernard had met in September 1927, probably at the coffee stall in Falcon Grove, Battersea. Bernard worked there, and Constance lived with her family in the same street. They had seen quite a lot of each other in the two weeks that they had known each other, going to the cinema or for walks. It had been a very innocent romance on her part; although he had wanted 'to go through her' (ie have sex), she was 'not that sort of girl'.

It is unlikely that Constance knew much about her new young man. If she had, she might have been a little less enthusiastic about him. Not that Sydney Bernard Goulter, to give him his full name, was all bad. He came from a reasonably respectable background. Born on 18 September 1902, he was one of six children and his father was a police inspector, based at Kingston and residing at Bockhampton Road from 1915–40. Some of his employers spoke highly of him. When he worked at *The Blue Anchor*, Weybridge, as a barman, in 1921, it was said he was 'a hard working and intelligent lad'. Another employer said he was 'willing and intelligent' and another thought he was a good worker when he was actually at work.

Bockhampton Road, 2009. The Author

Yet his life since leaving school aged fifteen was generally a troubled one. He had had a number of jobs, none of which lasted very long. These included, not only bar work in 1921, but also as an engineer at the Battersea Borough Electricity wiring and meter department (1919-20), at A C Cars Ltd, at Thames Ditton (1922-23) and in the Royal Engineers (1924–25). In August 1927, he bought a coffee stall franchise in Falcon Grove, for 10s a week, from Eleanor Lewis, of Parkham Street, Battersea, as said, though this didn't last long; and on 21 September he had given it up. One of his problems was that he was a very bad time keeper – frequently late or not turning up at all – and sometimes just walked out of jobs without giving any notice. Whilst in the Army, he annoyed his

Richmond Park. Author's collection

superiors by telling lies, being improperly dressed, disobeying orders, being absent without leave and other irregular conduct.

But it was not only his work pattern which was worrying. He was also a petty criminal with a number of convictions. In 1924, he was charged with impersonating a police officer and thus obtaining money from the public under false pretences, at Effingham. He was bound over for twelve months. In the following year, he committed a burglary at Gillingham and stole goods worth £14 17s. However, he was an incompetent burglar and left his army uniform behind in the house in Arden Street, which he had robbed. On another occasion, he stole a bicycle. He was given a two-month gaol sentence with hard labour in 1926, as well as being drummed out of the Army. It was not just crime that he was found guilty of; he was also served with a bastardy order, in January 1925, accused of making Miss Doris Halford of Deacon Road, Kingston, pregnant.

There were also problems at home. His mother, Sarah, said, in 1927, 'For the past five or six years he has been a source of trouble.' His father (by now retired from the police force) noted, 'For some time past I have had doubts as to the mental stability of my son, Sydney. He has seemed peculiar to me and seemed to have a generally morbid mind.' At one time, he took his youngest daughter to school himself, fearing she might be at risk from his son. His eldest daughter refused to go with Goulter to the Hippodrome on one occasion, to his great anger. In August 1927, he left home, living in lodging houses (in September 1927 he was living in a room in Church Road, Battersea, paying 8s a week to Samuel Fitzpatrick) and only returning home to have his dirty clothing washed. In late September, Sarah was worrying more about her wayward son, and said, 'I told my husband I could not stop in the same house alone as Bernard, as I was afraid of him.' He often followed his mother around the house. On one of his last visits there, at the end of that month, he stole a ten shilling note from his mother's purse.

We shall now return to Constance. Her life was entirely different to that of her lover. She was born in February 1906 and was from a working-class background. Her father, Edwin Oliver, was a lowly watchman and she was one of a family of ten children; six of whom still lived at home in 1927 and Constance was the eldest of these six. They lived in Falcon Grove, Battersea. On leaving school in 1920, aged fourteen, she began work as a typist at the British Steam Specialities, Tarnmill Road, Clerkenwell, and continued in that occupation from then on. She was healthy and behaved well, helping her mother in the house in the evenings and enjoyed singing and playing the piano. Occasionally she spent time with Mildred who lived nearby. It was said, she was 'highly respected at her place of business, and by all who knew her'. All in all, she was a steady worker and a model daughter – a great contrast to Goulter, indeed.

They had a short lived romance, yet in that time Constance had grown to love and trust Goulter. On Friday 30 September, they had arranged to meet on the following day at Putney railway station. They did so and went to the cinema, Putney Hippodrome. Goulter then saw her home. They then arranged to meet on the next evening, too. Therefore, the last time her family saw her alive was on Sunday evening, 2 October. She told her father that she was meeting her lover at Putney Station, telling him at 7 pm, 'I'm going to meet Bernard.' She had not introduced him to her family. She had not returned by 10 pm, which was very unusual for her. On the following day, her father found that she had not reported to her employers. He then reported her disappearance to the police at West Hill Police Station.

On Tuesday 4 October, Mrs Annie Martin, one of Constance's two married sisters, saw Goulter in Wandsworth High Street. She knew of her younger sister's romance with him and had seen her on the Sunday before she disappeared. Naturally, she was anxious and addressed him thus:

'Have you seen Connie?'

'No, and I don't want to,' was his reply.

Goulter seemed both startled to be asked such a question, and more than that, angry. But Mrs Martin persisted in her enquiry:

'You are the last person she was supposed to meet and its funny she hasn't been home. My mother is worried to death.'

'No, I was supposed to meet her at Putney Station about 7 pm, and she didn't turn up. I waited till 8 o'clock, and got fed up; and then went home to my mother.'

Whether Mrs Martin was satisfied by the answer given, we don't know. Perhaps not. Certainly, the next person to speak to Goulter found him to be in an odd mood. This was William Turbard, who knew of Goulter's romance with Constance. Goulter turned up at his friend's house that evening. Turbard thought that his friend was behaving oddly, and asked him, 'What's the trouble, Bert [he knew Goulter as Bert Randall]? you look very worried.' No answer was forthcoming and he asked Goulter to leave, which he did.

However, it was Charles Hicks, a park-keeper employed in Richmond Park, who played the next part in the unfolding drama. He later told the police:

> On the morning of the 5th October I started my duty at 9 o'clock. At 9.50 I was doing my usual rounds. When I was south of the middle road, near the triangle, I noticed something white in the bracken, which I took to be a dead

> deer. On approaching the object I found it was a woman. The woman was dead. Her right leg was drawn up.

The body was that of a young woman. She was lying on her back and her clothing was torn and disarranged. Parts of her body were exposed. A white cloth had been tied around her neck, with a knot on the right side. Her bloomers had been burnt and her arms were by her side. Hicks ran to find a passing motorist, who in turn fetched a policeman. PC John Frost was first to arrive, having been found by Robin Hood Gate. At 10.15 pm he was at the scene of the crime, and at 11 Dr Athelstane Nobbs, the Divisional Surgeon, had arrived. When the body was removed in the back of a police car because no ambulance was available, a number of articles were found near or under the corpse. There were five pieces of a broken umbrella, a hair slide, a fur necklet, a broken string of imitation pearls and a handbag with an empty purse. Clearly a struggle had taken place as the bracken all around the corpse had been trodden down.

It was also obvious who the victim was. Mr Oliver was taken to Kingston Mortuary to identify the body, which was that of his daughter. Later that day, Spilsbury and Dr Nobbs conducted a post-mortem examination. Death had occurred some time ago; at least thirty-six hours before the body had been found. Hence the murder must have occurred on Sunday or Monday. Oddly enough, Fred Cooper, another park keeper, had patrolled the park on the Monday and Tuesday and had not noticed the corpse, but then the park covers over 2,000 acres, so this is not too surprising. The time of death was indicated thus because rigor mortis had set in and insects were found on her hand and in her nose. There was a scalp wound on the head and marks around her neck. She had been battered by the umbrella and then had been strangled. She had also been robbed. The doctors concluded, 'It was quite evident from the general condition of the body, that before her death a fierce struggle had taken place.'

It was soon known to the police that Goulter had been seeing her. Once the police were aware of who they were looking for, they quickly got to work and patrols were dispatched in order to locate Goulter. Goulter's sister, on the instigation of her mother, had telephoned them to say that he had paid their home a visit earlier that evening. She had told Goulter, 'You cannot come in here, Bernard, you had better go to the police. Have you seen the papers, then?' Goulter had replied that he had and went to Richmond Park. Meanwhile, his father was summoned to Kingston police station, although he had offered to help his former colleagues. Yet they felt he had no intention of helping and would merely hinder their investigations.

It was PS Loring and PC Joseph Rogers who were in the patrol car which found the wanted man. They saw him at 9 pm standing at a bus stop on Kingston Hill, waiting for a bus to take him to London. It was a dark night, but they spotted Goulter by the lights of a bus. PC Rogers later recalled, 'I saw the accused about to board an 85 bus proceeding to Putney.' He was taken by the officers to Kingston police station. The two arresting officers were commended by their superiors thus, 'The officers referred to acted with great discretion, persistence and ability, with the result that what at first appeared to be a troublesome murder was satisfactorily cleared up by the arrest of the prisoner.'

Initially, Goulter said nothing to the police. Then he decided to make a confession, after he had been properly cautioned. He said that he had met Constance at 7.15 on Sunday 2 October at Putney station as arranged. They then took a bus to Richmond Park. Once at the park they entered via Robin Hood Gate. They strolled across to the Kingston Gate. They then sat in the ferns. He asked her to meet him on the following night, too. Constance had already seen him on the two last nights and as much as she loved him, did not see herself as exclusively belonging to him. She told Goulter that she was planning to go to the Lyceum with a female friend and a few other young people. A row followed.

Goulter then stated what happened next:

> I lost my head. I set about her. I hit her on the head with her umbrella which she was carrying – I hit her on the back of the head with the knob of the umbrella. She fell down, but

> did not go right out. She struck me in the face with her handbag and then I got hold of her by the throat, and held her until she was still alive, although she was in a very dazed condition. Her clothing, when I left her, was torn. That was torn during the struggle ... The fight we had was purely owing to jealousy on my part because she was going out with a girl on Monday, and two men.

He added, 'She put up a terrific fight, but I beat her at the end.' Before he left her, he tied a piece of white cloth around her neck so she would not regain consciousness until he was long gone, and stole her money from her purse – all of 2s 4 1/2d.

The police were convinced of the young man's guilt and concluded that he had 'brutally mauled' the deceased and that it had been a 'cruel and cold blooded murder'. They thought the reasons behind the crime were as follows, 'Goulter took the deceased to Richmond Park with one of two, or both intentions in his mind. It or they were to seduce her, or to rob her, or both'. It seems, though, that robbery was not the motive for the murder, but the one which Goulter gave them, namely jealously. In the next few weeks, the police sought additional information about the prisoner, writing to his former employers and enquiring about the mental health of his family.

Goulter was tried at the Guilford Assizes on 5 December. It had been thought he should have been tried at the Old Bailey because a London jury would not be biased against him, whereas a Surrey jury who had doubtless already read about the case in newspapers such as the *Surrey Comet*, might well be ill disposed against him. Goulter pleaded not guilty. His defence was one of insanity. It was said, 'The prisoner is a confirmed masturbator, and that masturbation is not uncommonly associated with many forms of mental disorder.' It was also noted that his great grandfather, George Henry Goulter, had suffered from mental ill health in his old age, dying at home in Kingston Avenue Road in 1882, and so had two other distant relations on his mother's side of the family. This type of defence, based on mental illness in the family of the accused, was not uncommon at this time – in 1926 a man accused of a murder in Catford was defended likewise (see the author's *Foul Deeds and Suspicious Deaths in Lewisham and Deptford*). However, in both cases, it was unsuccessful. The prosecution brought forward a number of eminent medical witnesses, such as Spilsbury and Dr Hugh Grierson, who countered such a defence. The prison doctor noted, 'The prisoner had not shown any signs whatsoever of insanity.' After twenty-five minutes of deliberation, the jury found Goulter guilty and the judge then passed the death sentence. Goulter sobbed and buried his head in his hands on the passing of the sentence.

An appeal against the verdict was made on 20 December, but all Goulter's barrister, Laurence Vine's attempts were in vain. After eighteen minutes the Lord Chief Justice turned down the plea and the sentence passed was upheld.

Goulter's last thoughts on the murder were as follows:

> I am very sorry I murdered the girl. I should like to offer my deepest sympathy to the parents of Constance and tell them how sorry I am for what I have done ... I did it because I was jealous.

Such regrets are not uncommon among killers, belated as they are. It seems that Goulter was an immature young man who was unable to control himself. He was also a very possessive and controlling man, who could not abide 'his' girlfriend to have a social life of her own. When she stood up to him, he used the only language he knew – violence – and, being physically stronger, was able to overwhelm her resistance to his assault. After having attacked her with her own umbrella, he then strangled her and left her to die – if she was not already dead – in the lonely park that night.

Goulter paid the penalty for his crime, by being hanged by the neck until he was dead, at Wandsworth prison, on 6 January 1928, at 8am.

CHAPTER 14

Murder in the Park (2) 1931

I sat with her for hours waiting for her to come round, and did not realise that I had killed her.

Richmond Park was not always a happy rendezvous for lovers and this chapter narrates a second deadly encounter. Yet the similarities with the previous chapter should not blind us to the differences, too. This story begins on a Sunday evening, 6 April 1931. Kathleen Wallis, of St James' Avenue, Hampton Hill, was a nineteen-year-old in domestic service, and was returning to her employer's house after seeing her parents. She was walking adjacent to Richmond Park at about 9 pm and later recalled:

> I was walking down a pathway which runs along the garden fence. About half way down the pathway to the road I stopped and heard a sound. I thought it sounded like someone trying to cry out, but unable to do so. My sister remarked that it sounded like a child. Just then the noise stopped. I looked towards from where the sound came and could just see a dark form. I saw a red glow which looked like a lighted cigarette. We both walked towards the road and again stopped but could hear no further noise. I then went to Kingston Gate. The dark figure did not move. I could not see if it was a man or a woman.

Later that night, a young man entered Kingston police station. He was in an excitable condition and made a most surprising statement. He said, to PS Gillespie, at 1.14am on 7 April, 'I believe I have done a girl in at Richmond Park.'

The young man was William Gordon Baldwin. He had been born on 31 January 1905, at Gibbon Road, Kingston. After

Gibbon Road, 2009. The Author

leaving school in 1919 he worked as a gas fitter for Kingston Gas Company. He joined the Army on 15 November 1920 and served as a private in the RAMC. During his military service, which included duty in Eygpt, he suffered from malaria. When he was discharged after his seven year service on 14 November 1927, it was stated that his record was exemplary. On 13 December 1924, he had married one Doris Hodgson at St Stephen's church, Paddington, and in the following April they had a son, Dennis. However, by 1930 they had separated by mutual consent, and whenever he was in work gave his wife small weekly sums of money. She lived in Clapham and then Kennington.

Baldwin was not in a good state. In July 1930, he lodged at Bessborough Street, Westminster, with one Louisa Green, his landlady. He was then briefly employed at the Army Clothing Store and claimed he needed money to buy his alleged girlfriend, one Daisy, from North Kensington, a present. He borrowed £7 from his landlady and then absconded. On 18 October, he went to his mother's house in Hampton and stole a wireless and clothing to the value of £29. On 19 October, he

Kingston Gate, 2009. The Author

took Lysol in order to kill himself, but failed. He explained, 'I bought the Lysol at Charing Cross. If a certain person had met me at 8 pm as previously arranged I should never have taken Lysol. I waited until 9.15 pm, the certain friend did not come so I made up my mind to do myself in and I will do myself in when I choose.' He failed and was admitted into Kingston Hospital where he was visited by his parents and left five days later. Dr Percy Davies later said of him, 'I noticed no signs of mental derangement.'

His victim that night in April in Richmond Park was forty-seven-year-old Sarah Ann Isaacson, who may have been Swedish in origin. She had been married in about 1911 to Frederick Albert Isaacson, but what was almost unheard of among working-class people; was allegedly divorced in 1917, though there is no record of this. She lived with her family for a few years, then she worked as companion to Mrs Polden at The Grange, Worcester Park, from 1925–27. She seems to have been single at this point as there was no reference to any gentleman callers. In April or May 1927, she began to work for Mrs Mary Fairbrother at the *Alexandra Hotel*, Park Road, Kingston.

The Alexandra Tavern, *2009.* The Author

Sarah met Baldwin when he began working at the hotel on 7 November 1930, as a potman. Although he was, 'honest, a good worker and always willing', problems arose. Baldwin, who did not reveal he was still married, fell in love with Mrs Isaacson. Matters came to a head early in the following year. Mrs Fairbrother noted:

> On Friday 6 March 1931, I had occasion to speak to Mrs Carr [as Mrs Isaacson was known] as to her being in Baldwin's bedroom. She made the excuse that she wanted to tell him something. I knew they were walking out together. Mrs Carr became very slack in her work and appearance and I thought they were rather too friendly and I decided to dispense with them both.

She was convinced that 'they had been having sex relations at the hotel' and gave them a week's notice, but they left on the following day. Baldwin soon obtained another job as a barman, this time at *The Prince of Wales* pub on Bridge Road, Molesey. This was on 16 March, but he chucked it on the

Richmond Park. Author's collection

following day, and rang his employer on 18 March to say that he could not come to work owing to being injured in a motorcycle accident. Mrs Isaacson went back to stay with her sister in law at New Malden.

In March, neither of the couple enjoyed good health. On 21 March, Mrs Isaacson went into Kingston Hospital for scabies treatment. On the following day, Baldwin was in Brighton. He was found by PC Prescott at 12.55 pm on West Street and appeared to have lost his memory, so was taken to the town's infirmary. Dr H J McCurrick later said:

> He was suffering from loss of memory. On admission he said that he had a blank in his nerves. He remembered heading home, but did not remember anything more until taken by a policeman to the town hall. He afterwards appeared to be quite rational, but could not fill in the blank in his memory referred to above.

He was discharged on 26 March to William Bland Tooting, his brother-in-law's care. He recalled, 'He seemed broody and disinclined to want to talk – he seemed nervous.'

The two were very much devoted to each other. Mrs Isaacson was visited in hospital on three occasions by Baldwin.

They also wrote to one another. In one of his letters, he wrote, 'You have made me so happy while I have been with you it has been the best time of my life.' She wrote, 'Seeing you today has taken 10 years off my life ... It is simply delightful to be here and know somebody loves you ever so much, really Billy darling it is just your love for me that has kept me young.' She was discharged on 6 April and went to Frederick Salveson's house in Malden Road, New Malden. He was her brother, and a respectable bank manager.

Emily Salveson was Mrs Isaacson's sister-in-law and she commented on her feelings for Baldwin. Mrs Isaacson thought he was thirty-four and a bachelor. Furthermore, 'I do know Baldwin brought happiness to her life and she was very much attached to him, in fact it was suggested that they should be married at Easter.' She added, 'She was very much infatuated', but thought she should break from Baldwin. However, on the day of her return, he rang her there and suggested they meet, to which she readily assented.

The two met at Waterloo station at 1.20 pm, and then went for lunch at the Coventry Street Corner House, before going to a nearby cinema. They then had tea. That evening they went to Vauxhall railway station and took a train to Malden. However, they continued onto Norbiton. At 9 pm they dined at *The Borough Arms* on Park Road. For old times' sake they took a look at their former place of work.

That night, Baldwin decided to tell Mrs Isaacson that he was married, and did so at the corner of Park Road and King's Road. The two then proceeded to Richmond Park. He said that she was feeling suicidal.

Returning to the scene at Kingston police station in the early hours of 7 April, the police went with Baldwin to the park and he showed them where Mrs Isaacson's corpse lay. It was fully dressed, and covered with the pages of the *Evening Standard.* There was an umbrella near her head and on examination, marks were found around her neck. On her body was a wedding ring, 6d in silver and 91/2d in bronze. Dr Armstrong, the Divisional Surgeon, was called.

When Baldwin was back at the police station, he made several statements as to what happened. One was the relatively brief, 'I took her by the throat with my hands and that is all I know.' He also said, 'I strangled her and then lost my nerve to do myself in. It was done at about 9 o'clock. I sat with her for hours waiting for her to come round, and did not realise that I had killed her.' He also said, on 8 April, to PC Hodge:

> I did not do this for the same reason as Goulter. We went to London and spent £2 and when we came back we only had 1s, so we made up our minds to die together. I strangled her and then lost my nerve to do myself.

Baldwin was searched and evidence of his poverty was found – there was only 9 1/2d on his person as well as three pawn tickets.

The inquest was held at Kingston on 10 April and Baldwin was accused of the murder by strangulation. He was sent to Wandsworth prison to await trial. At the trial, which took place at the Surrey Assizes, on 29 June 1931, the defence spent much time attacking PC Hodge's evidence. They argued that the crime was not Baldwin's fault, but was due to his suffering from amnesia. Yet Hodge stood up to his examiners and his superiors later noted, 'The PC is to be commended for the creditable manner in which he gave his evidence under stress of severe cross examination.' The jury took forty minutes to decide that Baldwin was guilty and so he was condemned to death. Despite an appeal based on insanity falling on 27 July, a reprieve was granted on 4 August and Baldwin was sentenced to penal servitude, for life.

There is no doubt that Baldwin and Mrs Isaacson went together to Richmond Park on the evening of 6 April. They were much in love, but were also despondent because they could not marry due to Baldwin still being married. They also had very little money. Did they enter a suicide pact as Baldwin stated? Very possibly, but the survivor of a suicide pact is deemed guilty of murder as Mrs Seddon discovered in 1905. At the Park, Baldwin strangled his girlfriend and, about three hours later, left her body and went to the police station to confess. He made no attempt to escape. The question is whether he was suffering from memory loss when he killed her. Quite possibly, as he had done so in the past. He was eventually given the benefit of the doubt and so had his life saved.

Chapter 15

Albert Hadfield – Guilty or Not Guilty? 1936

Let me find you in a better frame of mind tonight or there will be fireworks.

Albert Hadfield was a sixty-nine-year-old confectioner (he had been in this business since about 1921) who, in 1936, lived at Nelson Road, Whitton, near Twickenham. He had been born in Westminster, and lived much of his early life in south London, working as a clerk. He married Julia, at St George's Church, Southwark, on 9 October 1897. They had two children: Alfred (who was killed in the First World War) and Phyllis. Yet the marriage fell into difficulties. It seems that Hadfield, who had contracted a venereal disease in the 1890s, was deemed 'a man of exceedingly low moral character' and was 'most cruel to her'. She feared for her life. There was a separation order and his wife was given a 10s weekly allowance, which was paid irregularly. In 1911, he lived with his widowed mother, Clare, in Braybourne Avenue. He then lived with his daughter, who was his housekeeper. He also owned a house in Clapham. In about 1929, he had become acquainted with an elderly widow of independent means, Mrs Laura Eliza Mordaunt-Chapman.

From August 1927, Laura had resided on Hampton Road, Twickenham. She had been born in Usk, Monmouthshire, in about 1875, as Laura Davies. She had married a property developer called Algernon Mordaunt-Chapman who was twenty-two years her senior and from about 1908-11 they lived in Eltham Road, Lewisham, and from about 1919, Peak Hill, Sydenham. They had no children and her husband died in December 1922. She was still there until about 1926. Her nearest relation was Albert Davies, of Usk, her brother. She

Hampton Hill Road, 2009. The Author

had few callers and lived very quietly. She paid her bills regularly, was generous at Christmas to the tradesmen and was well known for ordering her drinks from *The Prince of Wales* pub. She owned twenty-one properties in and around London, the rents on these providing her with a monthly income of £218 19s, being paid by postal order. Although wealthy she had not made a will, though her wealth amounted to at least £13, 942 15s 11d. Hadfield helped her with her business matters, doubtless drawing on his previous commercial experience, and in 1936 was involved in helping her sell a house. He also wrote letters for her. On one occasion, he had helped her secure an income tax rebate worth £400, and was given 10% as a fee. He used to call on her every Monday morning.

The Prince of Wales *pub, 2009.* The Author

It was Hadfield who rang Twickenham police station at 12.35 pm on Thursday 9 July 1936, to tell them that all was not well with the widow. He asked, 'Will you please send an officer to this address? I think the place has been entered. The front door is open.' He suspected foul play because he thought her house had been entered illegally, and that there was a lot of clothes scattered about (clearly he had entered it, however briefly). He thought that her corpse might lie concealed under these. When the police arrived, they were greeted at the door by Hadfield himself. He took them to the kitchen and pointed to the window sill, where there was a note written on blue paper. He told them, 'I came yesterday and left that note, wedged in the window, as I had written two postcards which she had not answered.'

Twickenham Police Station, 2009. The Author

It was noticed that Hadfield was in an excitable condition and his hands were shaking badly. He then took the police upstairs – to the very place he had just come from – and showed them a heap of clothing in a bedroom. Something had been burning. Hadfield told them, 'You may find a body under there.' Sure enough, a foot could be seen portruding and once a blanket had been lifted up, the back and shoulders of a body could be seen. Hadfield seemed to be surprised and cried, 'My God! There it is!'

By the body were two postcards. Hadfield told PS Whapham, 'These are the two postcards I sent her. I want you to take charge of them as they will show you what I came here today for.' One was postmarked 7 July and the other for the following day and they both concerned letting a house. These seemed to be above board. Yet Detective Inspector Baker found another postcard in the bedroom. This was also from Hadfield, but was bloodstained. It was undated. There was a blurred fingerprint on it, of a thumb which had a scar on it. Hadfield's left thumb was similarly marked. Copies of the *Daily Express* for 7–9 July were found behind the doormat, whilst one for 6 July was located in the woman's bedroom, this pointing to 6 July being the day of the murder.

The widow had last been seen alive in her back garden on Monday afternoon, 6 July, by Mrs Alice Colledge, a neighbour. According to initial medical estimates, she had died between then and 8 July. Sir Bernard Spilsbury was called to examine the body, which was, of course, that of the late widow. He found numerous stab wounds on her back and neck, amounting to forty-six in all. There was also a bruise on her head and he surmised that she had been knocked unconscious and then repeatedly knifed. The item used to hit her was a heavy ornament which was found in the sideboard cupboard. Death would have resulted in fifteen minutes. He thought death could have occurred on either 6 or 7 July. The weapon used was not a penknife, but a weapon similar to a sailor's jack knife.

There was also an examination of the house. It seemed that the killer was probably known to his victim, because there was no sign of forced entry, on either the windows or doors. Nor was robbery a probable motive because sums of money were found throughout the house, and there seemed to have been no search for any valuables in the house. Under the wardrobe were ten £1 notes and other money and money orders to the value of £208. In the kitchen, a handbag contained £2 in notes, plus silver and bronze. Possibly the crime was caused because the killer wanted to destroy something which might incriminate him, as there was evidence that a pile of papers had been burnt, and these were found near to the body.

Police called at Hadfield's house, on 13 July, when he did everything he could to assist them. They were shown his clothing, including his cycling breeches and stockings, and his mackintosh. He told them that the breeches might show traces of creosote, as he had been creosoting the fence recently.

He emerged as the leading suspect. There was certainly some evidence against him. First, Mrs Florence Dickinson, of Bedford Road, Twickenham, had been waiting for a bus on Hampton Road on 6 July and heard a noise in Mrs Mordaunt-Chapman's house. She then saw a man nearby, who was cleaning something, but she could not make out his features. When she returned from her journey, an hour and a half later, she saw the same man coming out of the house by the side gate. She later identified him as Hadfield, whom she had seen before at his shop in Whitton. When seen in July 1936, he was wearing knee breeches and had a bicycle. She also saw him there on 8 and 9 July, but her identification of him may have been mistaken. A neighbour, Mrs Elkins, had seen Hadfield knocking on the door on 8 July, but received no reply. Hadfield denied he had been near the house when Mrs Colledge claimed he had.

As to motive, it was shortly ascertained that in July 1935, Hadfield borrowed £550 from Mrs Mordaunt-Chapman, at 5% interest, but he assured the police that he had kept up with the interest payments.

There was some other evidence against Hadfield. Firstly, his relationship with the dead woman was strained at times. Letters from him were located. Some extracts from them read as follows, 'I am very much surprised at your treatment. I have always been loyal to you.' Another read, 'I am worth my weight in gold to you the amount of money I save you.' Yet another read 'Why you wrote that scandalous letter I cannot imagine.' Another read, 'Let me find you in a better frame of mind tonight or there will be fireworks.' These comments suggest that Hadfield saw Mrs Mordaunt-Chapman as a difficult woman. Whether his annoyance at her perceived treatment of him could have led to violence is another question.

It is also worth noting Hadfield's remark about the victim, 'I don't know of anyone who she would even speak to, she was very eccentric.' He was perhaps the only person she saw regularly. The police made the following conclusion, 'He was the only person, as far as we can gather, who was ever admitted to the house. Of recent years and certainly he is the only person who had knowledge of this woman's habits and intimate affairs.' They thought Hadfield was guilty. It should also be wondered why Hadfield was at the house on Thursday – his usual visiting day was Monday. This was never explained and perhaps it was because, if he was guilty, he wanted to be on hand when the police arrived.

A man's bicycle was also seen outside the house on 6 July, at 1.10 pm, by William Humphries, a dustman. He said it was the same type as Hadfield's. Moreover, a milkman claimed he saw the figure of an adult in the house at 5am on 9 July.

The police deemed Hadfield to be a 'cool, calculating individual ... a man of patience and ability'. Other assessments of his character varied. One said, he was 'of quiet disposition and very honest'. A business rival thought differently, 'He seemed to be of very unfriendly nature'. The police concluded that the killer was either a lunatic or someone who had quarrelled with the deceased and that, 'The latter assumption appeared to be the more reasonable.' They had little doubt over whom that individual was.

The case for the prosecution opened at Brentford magistrates' court on 5 August and from then Hadfield was sent to the Old Bailey for trial a month later. However, both the prosecution and the judge concluded that there was insufficient evidence to proceed. The jury agreed with them and so Hadfield was found to be not guilty. A crowd of well wishers congratulated him, and he and his daughter took a taxicab home.

Although the police were convinced that Hadfield was guilty and one remarked after the trial, 'I think he is a very lucky fellow,' Hadfield would not let the matter rest. He began writing letters to Scotland Yard about the police's incompetence in failing to catch the real killer and in trying to pin the crime on him. For instance, in January 1938, he wrote, 'I am naturally personally concerned at hearing nothing of any effort to discover the perpetrator of this crime, you will admit I am sure, my right to be anxious, as I have been made to suffer and spend my savings to save my life, through the stupidity and inefficiency of your so called detective officers.' Hadfield named a neighbour as the guilty party, a man whom Mrs Mordaunt-Chapman was 'at daggers drawn'. But he was questioned and found not to have been involved. The police had to endure visits from Hadfield, but soon became annoyed by him and ceased to receive him, believing no good would result from these calls.

Another person accused was Mrs Hickling, of East Kirby, Nottinghamshire. In September 1938, one Cyril Harris claimed he was at Mrs Mordaunt-Chapman's house on 3 July and he said he saw the woman stabbing the widow to death. He was an inmate of a mental asylum and his claim was not taken seriously.

Her brother knew of no enemies of her sister. Albert and John Davies, farmers in Wales, inherited her money as next of kin. It eventually added up to £14, 635 8s after the estate had been resworn, but there is nothing to suggest that they killed to obtain it.

Whether Hadfield was rightly acquitted is another question. Certainly on the available evidence, it was right that he was given the benefit of the doubt, but circumstantial evidence is strong. Firstly, the killer had to be someone well known and trusted by the victim. Given that she had no known relatives or close friends in London, except Hadfield, this narrows down the number of suspects to him. Secondly, because nothing of monetary value was either taken or even searched for, the killer was evidently not a burglar. Hadfield had a financial motive: being in debt to her, and his character was none too good; and relations between them were strained at times. Perhaps there was someone else who had dealings with the victim, but as to who that was, we have no clue. Or perhaps Hadfield did kill her, then telephoned the police and made sure he was on hand at their arrival, to point out to them evidence that he had tried to call on her, unsuccessfully, in previous days. Yet for all the circumstantial evidence against him, there is no direct evidence, so whilst he may have killed her, the truth will never be known.

CHAPTER 16

A Middle-Class Murder 1937

Stand away from those panels or I will shoot you down like a dog.

Although much fictional crime in both books and on TV concerns the middle class, in reality, it is the poor who tend to kill one another. Of course, this is not always the case and this tale concerns a double tragedy among Richmond's middle class.

The Tribes seemed a fairly well-to-do, late Victorian family. The Reverend Odell Tribe was a clergyman, who had been the Congregationalist minister at All Hallows' church in Tottenham, until 1891, then became an Anglican and was ordained Vicar of St Ann's, at Brondesbury. He and his wife had several children. One of them was Naomi Tribe, born in

St John's College, Oxford. Author's collection

Ambulance on the Western Front, 1914–1918. Author's collection

1888 and the youngest was Maurice Odell, born on 4 June 1893, also in Tottenham. The early careers of both these young people began promisingly. Naomi was involved in hospital work in West London in 1909, whilst her brother attended Radley School (favoured by the sons of the Anglican clergy), Oxfordshire, from 1907–11. He then went to St John's College, Oxford, from 1911–14, reading Chemistry and gaining a BSc and beginning a career in metallurgy. He was also a member of the OTC there. In 1914, Naomi qualified as a surgeon, gaining her diploma of MRCS and her LRCP.

War changed both their lives. Naomi became resident medical officer at Great Ormonde Children's Hospital – a post reserved for men only, in the 1930s. But it was her younger brother for whom the war had a greater effect. He volunteered to join the army as so many others did. He was a stretcher bearer in the 8th London Field Ambulance, RAMC, at first, enrolling as a private on 2 September 1914, and then on 23 January 1915 as a second lieutenant in the West Riding regiment. He displayed great bravery in 1916 on the Somme, rescuing under enemy fire seven men, who had been buried by shellfire, but in doing so he was seriously wounded in the head by shrapnel, losing the sight of one eye. For this act of bravery he was awarded the Military Cross (gazetted on 4 November 1916 and receiving the decoration on 24 March 1917). He was also awarded a disability pension of £150 per annum because of his severe injury. Although there was a danger of him being returned to active service, despite his wounds, he was discharged. Although he remained on the army list until March 1918, he worked as a secretary and technical assistant in the Ministry of Munitions.

After the war, Naomi met Dr John Horace Dancy (whose father was also a doctor) at London University, where both were taking a year's course for the Diploma of Public Health. He was three years her junior, born in January 1891. Ironically, Dancy had qualified as a surgeon in the same year as her. After being at Warneford School, then King's College London, he had served in the RAMC in the war, as a temporary lieutenant, on 11 October 1914, and as a captain on 10 November 1915. He left active service in December 1916 and lived in Chiswick briefly, with his parents (now retired). After three weeks' acquaintance, Dancy married the shy and beautiful Naomi (in 1921), and they had three children, all of whom, by the 1930s, attended boarding school (the eldest boy, aged seventeen, was at Winchester, the other, aged fifteen, was at Repton and the daughter was at a Richmond boarding school).

Naomi did not – unusually – give up her career. The two doctors opened their practice over a boot shop on Erconwald Street, Shepherd's Bush. Two years later, they moved into a house provided by Hammersmith Council in Norbrooke Street, where their practice was rapidly increasing. They moved again in 1924, this time to Old Oak Road. When they left in about 1931, one Dr Spiro took over. John's health was failing and so they moved to Brighton, staying there until early 1936. They finally moved to a detached house in Queen's Road, Richmond, in about June 1936.

Naomi held a number of medical appointments. She did a great deal of lecturing, giving about 120 a year, especially on sociological questions. She held appointments at Tite Street (Chelsea) Children's Hospital and Bristol Children's Hospital. She was also the first woman doctor to be appointed to the Central Committee for Child Welfare at Carnegie House and was on the Central Committee of British Social Hygiene Council and was also an assistant medical officer of health for the borough of Hammersmith. She was a visiting physician at the Hammersmith Maternity Hospital, too.

After his distinguished war record, her brother held some well-paid positions, including those of secretary to the Handley-Page Aviation Company and secretary to the Government Disposal Board. He also worked as a clerk in an employment agency and as secretary to the Headmasters' Employment Committee (1919-22). He was a good public speaker and a brilliant wit, touring the USA as a lecturer. Until at least 1931 he was in employment with various organisations. He married Miss Dorothy May Heywood, a welfare worker, on 26 February 1921, living in a flat in Blomfield Road, Maida Vale. Tribe was also involved in voluntary social work and this was attested to by the Reverend Gill of St Augustine's church, Whitton. He said, 'He spent a lot of time in the East End, helping the under-dog and working at boys' clubs in the Bermondsey district.' He also held weekly meetings in his flat where men from different classes would discuss matters over tea and buns. It was known as Tribe's Den.

Yet there was a darker side to Tribe's character. This may have been caused by the injury he received in the war, which had left him with only one eye. Apart from the physical loss, he may have been mentally scarred too. It is not uncommon for a physical injury to lead the victim to serious crime in later life. One way of coping with this loss was to drink heavily. He also became very jealous of his sister; he envied her beautiful eyes, in contrast to him only now possessing one, and perhaps he also envied her successful career and happy marriage.

Tribe's health was a major problem in his life – and in those of others. In 1930, he had had a major operation on his head, to try and deal with the effects of his old war wound, and much bone tissue was removed. He was very sensitive about the matter and his sister-in-law, Rhoda Conder, said, 'He could not bear the thought of anyone looking at him. He had seen several specialists, but none had actually suggested he was insane, although he never seemed normal to me.' Tribe had often talked of committing suicide, but he had never threatened to kill anyone else. In 1935, he had spent three months in a private home for those suffering from nervous diseases. It was thought there that he was more of a danger to himself than others. Mrs Ada Dancy, his mother-in-law, remarked, 'Tribe had undergone operations and was becoming embittered. He was very intelligent, but his war wounds and the loss of an eye had changed him enormously. Under the strain, the sight of his other eye was failing.' Perhaps in light of all this erratic behaviour, in 1931, his wife and he had amicably separated and she was living on All Saints' Road, Bristol (he lived in a flat at Buller Square, Peckham). Yet the two still occasionally saw each other and went on holiday together. She often said she could take care of him, but he refused such help.

What perhaps made Tribe all the more dangerous was that it was thought that he might still have his old army revolver, a Smith and Wesson, in his possession, though there was some doubt over whether he had disposed of it or not. His wife though, knew he had kept it as a relic of the war.

The Dancys had done their best to help him. Under directions of an eye specialist, Dancy had been giving him eye injections throughout October and November 1937 at their house. This took place every Monday evening. This seemed to be going well. However, in early November, Tribe began drinking heavily again. On 12 November, his estranged wife appeared at his flat on Buller Square and found him in an unconscious state. He had been drinking. A few days later he rang Dancy and made threats against his sister. Miss Conder also told him about Tribe threatening his sister.

Although this was not unknown, Dancy was concerned. He drove over to Hammersmith, where his wife was working and was happy to find that she was safe. On Monday 15 November, when Tribe came around to their house for his injection, Dancy ensured his wife stayed the night at her mother's house, so she would not be in any danger from her brother.

Yet, such was Tribe's 'Jekyll and Hyde' nature, he soon changed his attitude towards his sister by 15 November. Dancy remarked, 'He had a very kind side to his nature and he was hurt that she was not there when he was. He was afraid that he had hurt her feelings.' On the following day, once Tribe had left the Dancy's home, he rang Dancy that night, in a very excited state, as he had been drinking, and declared how fond he was of his sister.

On 22 November, Dancy drove to Tribe's flat, following a traffic accident in which he had hurt his knees, in order to ferry him to their home for his weekly injection. He was then placed in two armchairs because of his injuries. On arrival, Tribe looked sheepish.

It is not certain exactly when this happened, but it was later alleged that Dancy gave Tribe a detective novel, *Murder in the House*. He also apparently gave him six 'indecent photographs', showing nude women in flagellation poses. All these were later found in Tribe's possession and Dancy remarked, 'Yes, he has always got trashy stuff like that.'

The drama came to a shocking climax in the early hours of Tuesday 23 November 1937. At about 11 pm on the previous day, Naomi returned from her work in a maternity clinic based in Westways Library. She and her brother had a row on her arrival. This was over an insurance policy which Tribe had taken out with Legal and General on her life in 1922, for £1,500 without her permission. He had paid the first premiums, but her husband took over shortly afterwards. Tribe had also received a commission for these. The final payment on the policy was due that week, and Tribe thought his sister's life should be reinsured, something he had been pressing her on for some time. Tribe threatened to kill his sister and her husband later recalled, 'For the first time I began to think he was really serious about it.' Yet Dancy was able to calm his brother-in-law down by making a joke out of it.

A new insurance policy covering the family for £5,000 had been taken out by Dancy. Tribe told him, 'Well, if that is the case you need not expect to live to draw the money' and then 'Anyhow, you can go your own way if you have left me out, but I think you are mean.'

His tired wife went to bed shortly afterwards. Her husband stayed up, and went downstairs to stoke the fire, just after midnight. He then went to the first floor to his study to type some letters to his children. He could hear his brother-in-law moving about in the room next door, and so he kept the study door ajar so he could hear what Tribe was doing. He thought it was silly of the man to be out of bed and in the cold when the radiators had been turned off. Dancy then went downstairs to stoke the fire again.

At 1.10am he heard Tribe go to the lavatory, and thought he had locked the door. Indeed, Dancy rattled the door, which was locked, and so, assuming that Tribe was inside, he felt relieved, because he no longer had to fear that Tribe might do something. It was then that tragedy struck, as Dancy later explained:

> I heard some [two] shots. I went to the door at once. My brother-in-law was coming from the bathroom which communicated with my wife's bedroom. I shouted at him, 'What have you done, Maurice?' He was advancing towards me with a revolver in his hand, pointing it at my head. 'Don't point that at me.' I could see that he meant to shoot me in the eye. I lolled against the door in a position of assumed ease, but all the time I knew there was a switch there where I could put my hand on it. When he stopped advancing, and I knew he was preparing to shoot, I switched the light out and dropped to the floor. He fired at me as I fell, dropping his aim.'

Dancy lay still, when Tribe turned on the light:

> He looked at me, and I groaned. He thought he had got me, so he slowly turned around to the lavatory and locked himself in. I immediately got up and banged on the door and said, 'Maurice, Give me that gun.' He said, 'Stand away from those panels or I will shoot you down like a dog.' I went into the bedroom to see what he had done to my wife. I felt sure he had hurt her. I did not know he was as bad as that.

Dancy then broke down the lavatory door and found Tribe hunched up inside. He had cut his throat with a razor and was dying. Dancy picked up the razor before replacing it. He also saw the revolver at his feet. Dancy then looked into his wife's bedroom and later recounted the terrible sight, 'I saw my wife in bed, she had been shot through both eyes and blood was spurting from one of her eyes.' He then summoned Catherine

Brooks, who had been housekeeper for thirteen years, shouting, 'Katie, come down, come down, he has shot my darling.' He then rang for the police. It was now 1.27am, just over a quarter of an hour since the shooting began. PS Ferne had been on duty that night when a call came to the station from the exchange, summoning them. He and PC Waddall arrived at 1.43am, and found Fireman Gibbs, who was also an ambulance attendant there. He told them that there were two corpses in the house. Dr Burn, the Divisional Surgeon, was then asked to come at once.

Ferne also went into Naomi's bedroom and saw a shocking sight:

> Mrs Dancy was lying on her back on the bed in night attire in the front bed room and apparently had been shot through both eyes while she was asleep. The bed clothes did not appear to have been disturbed.

Dr Burn saw her corpse and issued a death certificate. He noted that either of the two wounds would have been fatal. Both had been fired from the Smith and Wesson revolver that was found by Tribe's body. That revolver had been used to fire three shots. The third bullet hole was found by the window in Dancy's study, about four feet from the floor. The police took these away, and also found a bottle of methylated spirits and a bottle of crystals termed cocaine hydrochlor in Tribe's bedroom. Later, Dr Eric Gardner examined Tribe's body and, unsurprisingly, found it to be in a most unhealthy state. The liver was hard and fibrous, and there was disease of the kidneys and spleen. The cause of death had been the three wounds to his throat caused by his razor. Gardner commented on these, 'These wounds show evidence of, before commencing, of hesitation and uncertainty and exhibit all the characteristics of a suicidal wound.'

The inquest was held on Friday 26 November. Most of the evidence was given by Dancy, who described both the fatal occurrence and the events leading up to it. Rhoda Conder, Tribe's sister-in-law, also gave evidence about Tribe's health. As with Dancy, she attested to his 'Jekyll and Hyde' nature, and also paid tribute to the Dancys' kindness towards him. The jury returned a verdict of murder and suicide, committed when Tribe was insane. The police concurred with this view, one writing, 'There is no doubt that the dead man as a lunatic,' and another thought 'in my opinion it could only have been carried out by a lunatic'. Likewise, Tribe's widow said, 'he was very fond of his sister and must have lost his reason to harm her'.

There was much sympathy for the widower, and he received hundreds of letters, which he eventually replied to. There were also public tributes among the council and people of Hammersmith for whom she had done so much good work. The memorial service at St Catherine's church in Hammersmith, on Wednesday 24 November, was packed with civic leaders, former colleagues, and representatives of the many organisations she had been involved in. Sorrowful mothers from Hammersmith council estates also attended. The Vicar, the Reverend Beale, himself a close family friend, paid great tributes to her work, as might be expected. But he also made reference to her brother, too:

> If she were standing in my place today, she would ask, first, that you would extend to her brother the most merciful judgement that is possible. She would ask you to realise that he never, never wanted to go to war, that he went because he felt it was his duty. She would have you remember how, under heavy fire, he won the Military Cross, for having dug out seven of his men who had been buried by a shell. She would have you look upon this tragedy as one of the awful pieces of aftermath of the war, and realise that after twenty years, we have to bear the strain of tragedy and suffering of that war.

Naomi was cremated at Golders Green Cemetery on 26 November in a private ceremony attended by close family only. There were no flowers, because she had previously said that money spent on flowers would be better spent on feeding the hungry.

This had been a great tragedy, for Naomi Dancy appears to have been a most hardworking and popular woman, beloved of all who knew her, not least for her medical work, but also as a mother of three children. Lady Cynthia Colville wrote a piece espousing her virtues in *The Times*. Her brother, too, had been an intelligent and kind man, though his life and career had been blighted by the war and he never really recovered from his wound, which led to mental problems exacerbated by drinking in order to alleviate their symptoms. Perhaps it was because he had lost one eye and he envied his sister's beautiful eyes, perhaps as well as everything else she had, he deliberately shot out her eyes when he murdered her.

There are two intriguing footnotes to this terrible story. The first is that on 15 December, Dancy telephoned Dorothy L Sayers (1893–1957), perhaps the most literary of the female crime writers of the Golden Age of detective fiction and well known for her fictional sleuth Lord Peter Wimsey. It was a lengthy call. Part of it went as follows:

> 'I thought you might like to come and see the place ... it's quite a problem.'
>
> 'I'm afraid detective writers are rather stupid about problems in real life.'
>
> 'Oh, there's nothing to solve... But I thought you would be interested in hearing all the details.'

The author said that she was not well acquainted with the crime and that, though she occasionally spoke to members of the CID, they told her little about her cases. In the end she declined Dancy's offer (he suggested the two could meet after Christmas), pleading a prior engagement, and informed the police of the conversation. It does not seem that this offer was ever taken up, 'his offer seemed quite unnatural and inexplicable' thought the police.

Then there were at least two anonymous letters received by the police about the murder, both making a similar accusation. One read, 'I feel deeply that much has yet to be discovered'. It was alleged that this was not a simple case of murder, attempted murder and then suicide. Some thought that the

Queen's Road, Richmond, 2009. The Author

Richmond Police Station, 2009. The Author

murder was like something out of a book, and pointed to suspicious incidents. These were the finding of the nude photographs, the theatricality of Dancy's story about 'foxing' Tribe, the time lapse between Dancy's finding his wife dead and ringing for the police, the odd fact that he had picked up the razor from Tribe's hand before replacing it, and the fact that a new insurance policy, insuring his wife for £5,000 was taken out just before she died. A writer of detective stories or a conspiracy theorist could point to the fact that we have only Dancy's word that Tribe shot at him then killed himself, and that he could have killed his wife and then his unwell brother in law, in order to acquire the insurance money – perhaps, too he was envious of his brother in law's MC and his wife's successful career. Detective Inspector Howell made the following balanced assessment, 'There are many peculiarities and little suspicious incidents surrounding the case, but all the same, I think the verdict was the correct one.'

As a further footnote to the case, Dr John Dancy inherited £2,166 14s from his wife. He remained living at his house in Queen's Road until 1966, then retiring to Bournemouth. He never remarried and died on 8 December 1976, leaving £19,762 in his will.

CHAPTER 17

A Jeweller's Demise 1938

After a little while I managed to get the knife. At that time I think we were both quite mad.

Ernest Perceval Key was born in Beverley, Yorkshire, in 1872 and was the son of a Methodist minister and hosier and hatter, John Key, who was also born there. Ernest, who had at least three siblings, was apprenticed to a jeweller and a watchmaker. In 1901, he was an assistant jeweller, working in South Shields. In this year (on 8 January 1901 to be exact) he married Miss Rachel Maud Taylor of that town, whose father, Captain Jack Taylor, was a master mariner. They had at least three children (Gertrude, born in 1907, Jack, born in 1908 and Mormie, born in the following year). The family moved around various towns in Yorkshire, Key later managing jewellery shops in London. With the outbreak of war in 1914, Key, who was a crack shot, having competed at Bisley, taught musketry to volunteers in Sheffield. The family moved to Surbiton in 1916.

Key had many interests. He was a keen bowler and snooker player, and was a member of the St Mark's Men's Club and the Constitutional Club, too. He was a freemason, being a member of the Surbiton Lodge, where he had once been president, and also attended the Ditton Chapter. Spiritualism was another of his concerns, and most of the family were spiritualists, being members of the Surbiton Spiritualist Church and the equivalent in Tolworth. He was sober and moderate, respected and had not an enemy in the world.

At first the family lived above the jewellery shop in Victoria Road, Surbiton, where Key repaired watches and sold jewellery, but by 1933 they lived in Ewell Road. Key seems to have been a respected member of the community, but that did

Victoria Road, Surbiton. Author's collection

not prevent him from being safe from burglars. In March 1937, he lost goods to the value of about £300, a heavy loss indeed. This was all the more so because he could not get insurance. From that time on, he took his most valuable items home each night, a friend acting as bodyguard when returning home. By 1938 he was by no means a wealthy man, with his total estate being worth £185 16s.

On 24 December 1938, Key left home, at about 9.15–9.30am, a little later than usual, on his way to work. It was a cold and wintry day. At about 10.30am, he went to Alice Cooper's newsagent's shop, which was next to his. He rang Gertrude, his unmarried daughter. She later recalled that he said, 'I have rung up to tell you it is terribly slippery outside, in fact it is like glass … I slipped under a trolley bus but it was standing still. I'm alright.' He also warned Gertrude to tell her mother to be careful if she went outside. But Mrs Key became worried about her husband. Since 1930 he had suffered a stroke and two heart attacks. Soon afterwards, Key's son, Jack, was asked to go and see how his father was.

Jack Key was thirty years old in 1938. He had had a career in the music halls as a juvenile lead in comedy roles. However, an injury had finished his stage career and by 1938 he was running a mineral water business. Unfortunately it was not doing well, and only made him about £2 per week, so he sometimes assisted his father in the shop, especially during busy times after 3 pm.

Therefore, at about 11.30am he went to the shop. He was surprised to find that it was locked, so he went home to fetch a key. Ten minutes later, he inserted the key into the lock and opened the door. He later recalled the following:

> I opened the front door of the shop with a key, went through the shop to a room at the rear which is used as a workshop. I saw my father lying on his back on the floor. His head was towards me. There was a quantity of blood on the floor. His face, hands and his clothing were covered in blood. I unfastened his collar and tie and put my hand on his chest to try and feel if his heart was beating. I then went outside and telephoned for an ambulance.

Edith Smith, a nurse, was passing by and tried to assist. Although they had him taken to Kingston County Hospital, he died before reaching it. The time was about midday. Curiously enough, that was about the same time that another man arrived at the same hospital, having caught a taxi from Kingston railway station. Oddly enough, he was seen by the same man, who obviously had been assigned to deal with emergencies that day – Dr Louis Naz. This man gave his name as Charles Jackson, with a Norbiton address. He explained that the injures to his right hand were caused by a wood cutting machine. These took two hours to be dressed. At least they were not as bad as Key's fatal wounds. These were later described thus, 'There were something like thirty-one vicious stab wounds about the head, face and neck and sixteen or seventeen cuts on the hands. All must have been caused by a type of dagger or knife without a guard, so that the hand when delivering the blows might be cut.' Dr Gardner and Spilsbury conducted the post-mortem on 26 December.

Meanwhile, the scene of the crime was examined. There was a bloodstained bowler hat. It was size 7 and did not belong to the deceased man. Several items were missing. These included a gold watch and chain, a baby's silver rattle and a pair of Key's gloves. Key had left home that morning with between fifteen and twenty £1 notes. These were also missing. However, no fingerprints, except Key's, could be found.

The police visited laundries and dyers and asked if anyone had handed in any bloody clothes. They asked for anyone finding knives to inform them. Three youths found a bloodstained knife and handed it in. People as far afield as Nottingham and Leeds reported seeing suspicious characters.

Several witnesses helped the police reconstruct Key's last hours. Frank Armitage, an engineer, had been to the shop at 10.40am to buy a watch, but rang the bell and no one arrived. He left, but not before he had heard voices from within, and the message, 'Call back later, you will please.' Ten minutes later, Richard Whittaker, a teacher and a friend of Keys, saw Key talking to a woman. This was Ada Archer, who was placing an order for earrings at 10.45-10.50am. Major Louis Weigall passed the shop just before 11 and saw Keys there. However, when Joseph Bone, a bank messenger, passed the shop at 11.25am, he found it was shut.

The man initially suspected was Jack Key, by his 'manner and demeanour', but what these were, the police file does not elaborate. Perhaps it was because he had discovered the body and because he was short of money. Yet he was rapidly discounted.

Others came forward with useful information about the man the police wanted to speak to. On 28 December, Bertram Patient, manager of a pawnbrokers on Kew Road, Richmond, recalled refusing to accept a gold watch for pawn on the evening of 24 December, and described the man in question. Robert Woodhams of Twickenham had also seen a man with a bloodstained overcoat on that day and told the police at Twickenham police station. Another witness was thirteen-year-old Dorothy Harris who recalled seeing a man with injured hands in Middle Lane, Teddington, at 4.30 pm on the day of the murder, who asked her to count a wad of £1 notes.

The description of the man was circulated in the press and on the BBC on 29 December. A man who fitted the description had bought a doll's pram for £1 12s 6d from a shop on Hampton Hill, at 8.45 pm on Christmas Eve. Other shopkeepers came forward with similar stories.

It was DC Maudsley who recognised the wanted man as a neighbour of his. This was William Thomas Butler, who had been born on 27 January 1910. Until he was nineteen he lived with his mother. He had attended St Mark's School, Tolworth, leaving on 17 November 1919, then going to the council school on Stanley Road in Teddington, which he left on 10 February 1922. For the next few years, he worked for his uncle Albert, a greengrocer, of North Road, Teddington. Yet his criminal tendencies emerged in 1927 when he was bound over at the county Quarter Sessions for housebreaking and receiving stolen goods.

This did not prevent his getting married to Eveline Muriel Cook in January 1929, whilst not yet twenty. The marriage led to two daughters, Patricia aged five and Jane, aged eight, by 1938. His employment career was unsteady in the 1930s. Mr Wood, a grocer, of Walton Road, east Moseley, employed him as an assistant from 1935 – July 1936. Mr Boxall employed him from February – July 1937 in Worcester Park, in a similar position. Then he worked as a grocer's assistant and chauffeur to Mr Stewart, a greengrocer of Fulham, from August 1937–February 1938. Butler was not such a bad worker, it being said of him, 'Butler left all these places of his own accord and though described as normal and fairly satisfactory, he seems to have been rather restless.'

Yet he was now unemployed. The family now lived at Laurel Road, Hampton Hill and because his wife was obliged to go out to work, he felt terribly upset. Furthermore, one of his daughters was taken ill. In October of that year he had begun a new career – that of burglary, operating in Greenford, Brentford, New Malden and Hounslow. In all he broke into seven houses in the next two months. Some of the stolen goods were sold to a Hammersmith jeweller. Others were allegedly sold to Key.

Butler was visited by the police that day and taken to Kingston police station, though he first said, 'I know nothing about it'. At first he said that on that day he had been knocked down by a motorcyclist on Ham Road, Richmond. The man was about to go on holiday, and did not want to be entangled in any drawn out official procedures. So he gave Butler £15. Butler then went to Kingston Hospital, pretending to be the forementioned Charles Jackson, where he claimed he gave incorrect information at the hospital because he could not afford the medical fees (despite just being allegedly given £15). He said that he was nowhere near Mr Key's shop and was not even in Surbiton on that day. The police were unconvinced. Several people, including the shopkeepers who had served him on that fatal day, disproved his story about his movements on 24 December, four out of eight picking him out of an identity parade. Furthermore, £1 notes were found on his person. He had pawned the gold watch and chain. The baby's rattle, bloodstained, was found at his home and the hat found at the scene of the crime was also found to have been his.

So Butler gave a second version of events. He said, 'I did not tell you the exact truth. I was there, but I did not enter the shop.' He alleged that a 'Detective Reeves' had employed him on that day to drive a car for them. Apparently his employer had borrowed his light coat and then entered Keys' shop. The man then returned, wearing a different coat, having the other rolled up. They then drove to a lonely lane in Esher Common. Butler was then forced to wear the coat and was given £10. Inside the garment was a gold watch, which he later pawned. The injuries to his hands were caused by his slipping in the road and clutching bicycle wheels, and he had told this tale to his mother and his mother-in-law, Mrs Cook, both of whom lived in Teddington. There was no one called Detective Reeves and this name appeared on 13 visiting cards found on Butler's possession. It was discovered that Butler had had these cards printed at J H Broad's shop in Richmond. The description of the car and its registration led police to believe it was from Cheshire originally, but no such car could be traced, despite nationwide enquiries.

Then there was a third account given by Butler. At 9.15am on Christmas Eve, he left his home with Patricia, and took her to his mother-in-law's house at Middle Lane, Teddington. He left her there, saying he needed to collect his wages and then do some shopping. He took a trolley bus to Kingston, alighting at

Kingston Bridge. Author's collection

the bridge. He then went to Brighton Road and entered a barber's there. As it was very busy, he left without having his hair cut. Butler then went to Victoria Road and recalled, 'Mr Key and I knew each other very well, as we have had several dealings together and directly he saw me he invited me round to the back of his shop as he normally does.' It was just after 11.

He continued:

> He owed me about £15 to £20, the balance on different things I had sold him. I went to the shop and asked him for the money. He said I could not have it, as he was short of cash. I told him I would not go until I had it. We stated to quarrel and suddenly he turned round to the bench and took up a knife. He raised the knife to strike me. I made to grab his wrist, and caught hold of the blade. We had a terrible struggle. My hands were bleeding ... After a little while I managed to get the knife. At that time I think we were both quite mad. Suddenly Mr Key collapsed on the floor. I was striking at him with a knife before he collapsed. I knew Mr Key always kept his money in his trouser pockets, so I felt in them and took out about 10 or 12 notes. I took my overcoat off, which had blood on it, and put his overcoat on ... I then went out, pausing to take a little box of rings and a baby's rattle. I took them to get my money which Key

owed me. I did not think he was hurt so badly. I did not know he was dead until the next morning.

That afternoon, after buying a new bowler hat on Eden Street, Kingston, he went to the railway station and had one Charles Steward drive him to the hospital, as already stated. At 2.30 pm he visited his mother, at King Edward Grove, Teddington, then went to Mrs Cook's house in Middle Lane (it was here where he met the little girl as noted above). That evening, he tried to pawn a gold watch, but the first shop refused and redirected him elsewhere. He made £6 from it in a shop in Brewer's Lane, Richmond, then went on to make other purchases. Apart from children's toys, he also bought a new suit.

The question as to whether Key was a receiver of stolen goods was investigated. Naturally, his son denied this. However, one Blythe Keats, a burglar, said that in 1931 he had heard from another thief, one Peacock, that Key was a receiver. Yet the police noted, 'All the property found in the shop of the deceased and all the old gold at his private address was shown to each of the losers without a single item being identified.' There was an instance on 28 April 1938 when a youth had brought jewellery to sell to Key. Key refused, saying he needed to see a letter from the lad's father first. On the following day, the boy did so – it was a forged one – and Key then bought it, returning it to the real owner when asked. The police noted, 'This instance demonstrates the careful manner in which Mr Key conducted his business.'

Butler also told the police where he had hidden the knife, a bloodstained coat and various items he had stolen. He had taken them to a deserted house in Portsmouth Road, Kingston. The rings there were identified by Jack Key as having belonged to his father. The knife had been sold to Butler on 19 December 1938 at a shop on Paved Court, Richmond and Lawrence Chitty, a shop assistant, recalled the purchaser. The weapon was eight inches long and the four hairs attached to it matched Key's.

He pleaded not guilty and on 18 January was committed to trial at the Old Bailey.

At the trial, the defence argued that Butler had been provoked by Keys and that the killing had taken place whilst his passions overrode his restraint. He struck only in self defence. This was a case of manslaughter, not murder, therefore. On 16 February, the trial was concluded. The jury discussed the case for fifty minutes before returning their verdict. Although one of the women was in tears, they decided that Butler was guilty. Mr Justice Singleton passed the death sentence on Butler. Superintendent Beck commented, 'Butler gave evidence on his own behalf but made a poor show, particularly when he said he was not sorry for the deed.' He also added that the self defence argument 'was quite unsupportable having regard to the number of wounds found on the deceased'.

The case was taken to appeal on 13 March. But there were no grounds for altering the conviction and so the appeal was dismissed. The Home Secretary saw no reason why he should grant a reprieve. On 29 March 1939, Butler was hanged at Wandsworth prison.

The question is, why did Butler go to Key's shop? If Key was not a receiver of stolen goods, as appears likely, presumably Butler thought he might be. He may have made an offer of the goods he had stolen. What did Key do next which led to a fatal attack? Did he threaten to call the police? If so, that would be a reason for Butler to attack him, using the knife he had bought. We know that Butler was lying when he said that it was Key who had the knife and attacked him, so this hypothesis seems possible, as well as showing Butler's story of self defence to have been a nonsense. Possibly it was a case of attempted robbery, with Butler taking a knife as a method of frightening the older man into handing goods over to him. Or perhaps he meant to kill him anyway, and then rob the shop. We shall never know what exactly happened just after 11 in that shop on that morning of Christmas Eve, 1938.

The case gained international fame, with German newspapers reporting that a spiritualist had been used to solve the case. This seems to have been a mistake due to Key's interests in spiritualism and had no foundation in fact. There were also touches of the macabre. Dr Roche Lynch was allowed to retain Key's bloodstained jacket for lecturing purposes and the knife used to commit the crime was kept for Scotland Yard's Black Museum.

CHAPTER 18

The Second Death on Kingston Hill 1939

The old bastard has got what he deserves.

Kingston Hill, as already noted in chapter 8, was where many of Kingston's wealthier residents lived in their detached houses adjoining the east side of Richmond Park. Theophile Jean Baptiste Desnos, aged sixty-seven in 1939, was one of these fortunate people. He was probably of French parentage, but had been born in Bermondsey, London, in 1872 and was living in New Cross Road in 1901; and was then working as a manufacturing chemist. In 1911, still with the same occupation and still single, he lived with his two servants, at Lancaster Place, Richmond. By 1939, he lived at The Beeches (a detached house, now demolished, on the east side of Kingston Hill, nearly opposite to the Knoll), with his wife, Winifred Ida Desnos and their daughter. Desnos' wealth stood at £22,255 2s, a very large sum indeed (worth about £823,000 today), and he was described as being in the import business. They had lived there since about 1932. They also had several servants. The latter included, from 1 October 1938, George John Brown, a gardener, and his wife, and Richard Clarke, a chauffeur. The Browns lived in a flat above the garage.

Brown was one of seven brothers who fought in the First World War, and of these, five were killed in France. Brown was in the Black Watch regiment for two years. After the war, he and two other men worked on a farm near Nottingham. He worked for the Duke of Buccleuch at one time, and from late 1936 until October 1938 he worked for a Mr Beaver of Kenley. All his employers stated that he worked satisfactorily, he always left his jobs of his own accord, but that he did have a violent temper.

Kingston Hill, 1900s. Author's collection

It is probable that Desnos had not sought a reference from one Miss Mabel Grigsby of Little Meadow, West Drayton, Middlesex, whom had employed Brown in 1936. Whilst working there, he had struck a fellow gardener, one Mr Hart, with a cane, and had shook his employer. Apparently he had told his employer that his colleague was very slow, and so she should either sack him or he would kill him. Thinking Brown was jesting, she ignored him. On both counts, Brown was angry that they were doubting his integrity. Brown was clearly of an explosive temperament and woe betide anyone who crossed him.

A deadly explosion occurred at The Beeches, and was described by Clarke thus:

> At 9.30 am 25 March 1939 I was in the kitchen of the house. The accused [Brown] came rushing through the kitchen. He said to me 'I have knocked the old man out and he lays in the garden. You had better go and see to him.' He then asked where the bloody women were. He said, 'Where are the bloody women? I am going to serve them the same.' He said, 'The old bastard has got what he deserves.' He went through into the hall and up the stairs.

Clarke went out onto the veranda and saw the immobile form of his employer lying there. He was lying on his back and his glasses were broken. Blood flowed from his cheek and he was unconscious. There were two Greek statuettes near to his head. Mrs Desnos soon appeared on the scene, and then Brown arrived. He struck her twice on the head, and when Miss Desnos came there, she was shaken by him, too. She ran away and her mother went to her husband. All this happened so quickly that Clarke was unable to intervene.

The police came to the house and took Brown into custody. PC Cosh noted that Brown 'was agitated'. Dr Alex Wilson, of Putney Hill, arrived at 9.45am to examine the injured man. He had him removed to Putney Hospital. They spoke to Clarke about the affray. He said, 'I have not noticed any previous trouble between Brown and Mrs Desnos. I knew of a dispute about Mrs Brown's money … I did not think Brown would do such a thing as strike his employer.'

Brown explained that 'I had an argument over some money'. Apparently, Mrs Brown was paid 10d per hour, but her insurance stamps were not paid for her by her employer and her husband was angry about this. However, he also said, 'The root of this trouble is that he refused to pay my wife for the work she has done in the house, she has worked hard and he refused to give her anything and that is what the row was about'. In the argument between the two men, Brown claimed, 'He called me a libellous cad and I struck him. I will do it again'. He added, 'I wish I had killed him,' but then said, 'I didn't hit him with any malice.'

Desnos' condition was severe because he had had a thin skull. He did not get better and so an operation was carried out. Unfortunately it was not a success and he died on 30 April. Spilsbury was called on to undertake a post-mortem on 2 May. He concluded, 'The cause of death was fractures to the skull, haemorrhage around the brain and acute bronchitis and bronchial pneumonia … The deceased received a blow with some blunt instrument which caused the depressed ferule.' The blunt instrument in question was one of the statuettes which had been found by Desnos. Brown was charged with murder and manslaughter.

At the magistrates' court Brown was sent to the Old Bailey for trial. Meanwhile he was sent to prison and was examined by Dr Hugh Grierson, the prison's medical officer and a man with much experience of dealing with prisoners. Grierson reported as follows:

> There is no history of mental disorder in his family, neither is there any personal history of such ... At no time has he shown any evidence of mental disease or disorder.

Although 'circumstances may arouse a violent temper' in him, and he was 'of the paranoid type', he was not insane and was thus capable of standing trial. Brown's previous instance of violence in 1936 was also discovered.

The trial took place on 16 May 1939. Brown was found not guilty of murder, but guilty of manslaughter. He was sentenced to twenty-one months' imprisonment, and the leniency of the sentence was due to the fact that he had not used a weapon to strike Desnos. It seems that that he was knocked over and then hit his head on a statuette, which resulted in his death, making this an accidental death, not a murder. Mrs Desnos remained living at The Beeches until about 1951.

CHAPTER 19

Why did Jack Martin Commit Matricide? 1948

I don't know what I done with the iron. I don't know why I did it. I came over queer.

Several of the chapters in this book have posed the classic murder mystery question – whodunnit? This one, by contrast, poses the perhaps more difficult question – whydunnit?

Jack Martin seemed to be a very ordinary sort of fellow. He had been born in 1922 and, after leaving school, worked as a labourer for several local firms. He was called up for military service during World War Two, in the General Corps of Signals, the Royal Corps of Signals and finally the Royal Army Ordnance Corps. Throughout his service he remained a private and suffered from mild deafness. Martin never served abroad. He was demobbed in July 1947 and was given an excellent character reference, it being stated that he 'has carried out his duties conscientiously and well … honest and respectful to his employers. He should prove a useful asset to any civilian employer needing a capable and hard working man'. He returned home and soon found work. In 1948, he lived with Emily, his widowed mother (aged sixty-two), and his two other bachelor brothers (Albert and Leonard, both of whom were older that he). They lived in a house on Cambridge Road, Kingston. He was also single and worked as a labourer.

At 11.15 am on 6 April, Mrs Lillian Bowyer, of Bonner Hill Road, Kingston, and a daughter of Mrs Martin, arrived at her mother's house. She had called to see her mother, but instead, on entering the kitchen, was shocked to see Jack's body with a gas ring in his hand. Smelling gas, she turned it off and opened the windows. Her husband, George, was close at hand. He rendered first aid to his brother-in-law and found he was still breathing. They then called the emergency services.

Cambridge Road, 2009. The Author

The police arrived at the house at 11.42 am to find Martin unconscious and suffering from the effects of coal gas poisoning. He was taken to Kingston Cottage Hospital, where he began to recover. When he did so, he told Detective Inspector Findlay the shocking news, 'I killed my mother'.

Soon after these dramatic words were uttered, the police made their second visit of the day to the house in Cambridge Road. Findlay later described the following scene:

> I found the body of an elderly woman in a cupboard under the stairs of the living room, reclining on coal. The body was clothed and there was bloodstains on the face and hair. There was no disturbance in the coal cupboard. It was apparent the body had been placed there after death ... Examining the room, I found a piece of carpet rolled up, and on a chair near the cupboard upon which were bloodstains. There were several spots of blood on the floor covering near the door leading from the living room to the front room.

The corpse was that of Emily Martin. Dr Francis Camps, a pathologist (who was later involved in the Christie/Evans case), examined the body at the mortuary that evening and concluded that death was due to manual strangulation, adding that there was a scalp injury caused by a flat iron. A cloth had been found in the scullery, with bloodstains on it, and presumably this had been used to wipe marks from the floor where the body initially lay before being moved to the coal store.

Naturally, Martin was questioned about what had happened, and he showed no reluctance to tell all he knew; and on being told he would be charged with murder, replied, 'Let's get on with it.' He told Findlay:

> I didn't go to work this morning because I didn't feel too good. I got up about half past seven. Mother was up and I told her I didn't feel too good, so she said, 'Go and see Dr Childs.' I had some breakfast and mother went up to the meat shop. I was still indoors when she came back from the meat shop. I had a flat iron in my hand and she turned her back on me near the coal cellar door and I hit her on the crown of her head with it. She was just going down and I grabbed her round the neck. She went on the floor near the door that goes out from the kitchen into the front room. She was lying on her back and I strangled her with both hands. Then I picked her up and put her in the coal cellar. I washed the floor over a bit with a rag from the sink and pulled a bit of carpet over a bit. I don't know what I done with the iron. I don't know why I did it. I came over queer. Then I went over 'The Duke' had a pint of beer and went back and put my head over the gas ring. When I came round I was in hospital. I wasn't too bad, then. It all seemed such a long time ago.

The police questioned other family members about Martin. The crime seemed inexplicable. He was not known to harbour any ill feelings towards his mother. As Frederick, a brother of his, told them, he had 'never heard Jack use a bad word towards his mother, with whom he was on good terms'. Yet they all agreed that he was not quite himself. George Martin stated, 'Jack has been having queer spells for about the last three months. He seems to have suffered from fits of depression, would appear vacant and never speak to anybody.' Bernard Shepherd, a brother-in-law, added, 'He then appeared unsettled and at times had a vacant look about him. He would sit and stare and glare and not say a word.' George Bowyer made similar comments and referred to the 'vacant look'.

Clearly, Martin was suffering from ill health, but it is unclear exactly what this was. There was no history of mental illness in the family, though he had complained of headaches recently. In the previous August he had been suffering from jaundice and in November he had shown signs of developing an inferiority complex. During his military service, which had only recently come to an end, it had been noted that he may have had sexual problems (these were never specified; possibly homosexuality was being hinted at).

Martin pleaded not guilty but reserved his defence when brought before the local magistrates on 23 April. He was tried at the Surrey Assizes on 7 July 1948. He was found guilty – there could be no other verdict and there was no doubt that he had killed his mother. However, because of his questionable mental state, he was reprieved from execution and was sent to Broadmoor. On 27 April 1972 he was discharged.

Why had he killed his mother, against whom he had no quarrel? Findlay gave the following answer, 'I am of the opinion Jack Martin has some form of mental black out. He is a peculiar type of fellow ... he was on good terms with his mother and there was no ill feeling in the house.' It is unfortunate that the police file on this case does not include a psychiatric report, as would have to have been undertaken to assess whether he was mentally capable of standing trial. This would have provided further clues to why Martin killed his beloved mother. As it is, we may never know the answer, but those with an understanding of mental health issues are clearly well placed to hazard a diagnosis. Dr Rossiter Lewis, a Harley Street psychiatrist, claimed it was schizophrenia. He said that Martin had suffered a short period of acute mania, being deluded to believing he was being threatened by the world and by his mother in particular. So he killed his mother, believing her to be a malign influence working against him. Dr Matheson, prison doctor at Brixton, agreed with this, stating that Martin knew what he was doing, but did not know that it was wrong. All we can be sure about is that this was not a premeditated crime, it lacked motive and once it had been committed, the killer felt remorseful and tried to take his own life. When this failed, through the intervention of his sister, he was all too ready to confess to the police without any hesitation. Findlay's layman's assessment of the situation does not seem too far off the mark – Martin suffered a very temporary mental aberration in which he committed a terrible act.

CHAPTER 20

The Teddington Towpath Murders 1953

I must have a woman. I cannot stop myself. I'm not a murderer.

The year was a memorable one. The Queen was crowned. Everest was climbed. Ian Fleming's first James Bond novel, *Casino Royale,* was published. From the point of view of London crime, John Christie strangled his last three victims, and later that year was arrested, tried and hanged. Three of his other victims were found in Rillington Place and questions were asked whether his fellow lodger, Timothy Evans, had been rightfully hanged for another two of the murders committed there. This alone would have made 1953 a memorable year in the annals of crime. Yet there were other despicable murders in that year. These were not like the ones committed by Christie, in the inner London slums. These were perpetrated in the outer suburbs. As Sherlock Holmes remarked, 'the lowest and vilest alleys in London do not present a more dreadful record of sin than does the smiling and beautiful country-side'.

North Surrey was not a safe place for women in 1952–53. It all began on Oxshott Heath, on the early afternoon of 25 March 1952. A married woman (whose name has been blacked out in the police file) was attacked on Oxshott Common by a man whom she did not know. She was knocked on the head and dragged off before being assaulted. There was another attack on the morning of 24 May 1953, when fourteen-year-old Kathleen Ringham of Albany Crescent, Claygate, went for a walk. She was attacked by a man armed with a chopper and was sexually assaulted. At least these two escaped alive.

Others were even less fortunate. One was Barbara Songhurst (born 19 April 1937), aged sixteen, of Prince's Road, Teddington, an assistant at Harwood and Hills, a

Oxshott Heath. Author's collection

chemist's shop (where she was paid 35s per week) on Hampton Hill. The other was her friend Christine Rose Reed (born 18 March 1935), aged eighteen and of Roy Crescent, Hampton Hill, and a factory worker (paid £3 18s 9d per week). They were spending Sunday 31 May 1953 on their bicycles, riding along the riverside. They were later described as 'virtuous clean living girls both very fond of dancing and of the company of boys'. Barbara, who had attended Victoria Girls' School, Princes Terrace Road, Teddington, leaving at fifteen, was one of a family of seven and her father was an invalid. The house where she lived was poorly kept and she was allowed to stay out late at nights. Christine was referred to as being 'rather mentally backward'. She had two siblings and her father was a grocer's assistant. Unlike Barbara, she came from a well ordered home, but like her, was allowed to stay out until late.

On the previous night they had been with Joy Woolveridge, and had been at York House, Twickenham, at a dance. They returned to Christine's home at 12.45 pm. They left the house after breakfast to go to Barbara's. Joyce went home at some point. The other two went out for a cycle ride, returning to

York House, 2009. The Author

Christine's home for lunch at 2 pm. They returned for tea at 5 pm and then left again, being at Christine's house from 7–7.30 pm.

Much of their day, and certainly all the evening, from 8 pm, however, had been spent with three lads at their riverside camp, at Ham Meadow, not far from Teddington Lock. One of the youths was John Alan Wells, of Roy Grove, Teddington, aged twenty-one. He had known Barbara for six weeks and Christine for five years. His companions were Albert Edward Sparks and Peter Raymond Warren. They had talked and kissed, but there had been nothing more than that. The girls left the camp at about 11.30 pm that night and rode on the towpath towards the lock. Only one man ever saw them alive again.

The Thames at Richmond. Author's collection

On the following day, Barbara's corpse was fished out of the river by PS George Hays. She had been floating on the Thames near to Water Lane, Richmond; clearly the ebb tide of the previous night had washed her that way. It was George Coster, a fifty-three-year-old, employed by the PLA (Port of London Authority) as a foreman, who first saw her; he initially thought the corpse was that of a boy. Her mother, Gertrude, identified her. Although there was a wound in her head, she had been stabbed to death after having been assaulted. Her shoes were missing and there was no sign of her bicycle. Blood was found on the towpath near to the Teddington Locks, which were about a mile and a half from where her corpse had been found. Upon investigation this was found to have been from two blood groups. Two pairs of girls' shoes were also found here. There was no sign of her friend, and police issued a description of her. Police launches began to drag the river and grass near the verges was mowed in the hope that a clue might be found.

The police continued their searches on the following days. Open land near to the river as well as that adjacent to the towpaths were examined, dogs being used, as were mine

Teddington Lock, c1900s. Author's collection

detectors. A charred waist coat and blue serge trousers were discovered. More usefully, on 2 June, Christine's bicycle was located at the entrance to the lock gate, about 100 yards from the spot where the crime had occurred. Chief Inspector Herbert Hannan, who was put in charge of the investigation, began questioning anyone who might be able to help. These included American Air Force personnel from their base in Bushey, and about fifty people who said that they had seen the girls on Sunday. An eighteen-year-old leading aircraftsman in the RAF who knew the girls was sought. House-to-house enquiries were made, including among the large estate at Ham, in order to ascertain the whereabouts of the adult male occupants and for anyone who had seen the girls. Malcolm Else, who was questioned, was from Newcastle, and he had been in Richmond on 31 May, seeing his fiancée, but he could not shed any light on the crime.

The inquest on Barbara was set for 4 June, at Kingston, but was postponed. Meanwhile, the police considered applying to the Port of London Authority to have the river drained from Teddington to Richmond weir. This was granted and led to, on Saturday 6 June, Christine's body being found, near

Duke's Hole and Glover's Island (about a mile upstream from Richmond Bridge). As with her friend, there were blows to the head, but it was the multiple stab wounds to the body which had caused death. The sexual assault on her took place after death. There was also an injury to her arm, suggesting that she had tried to defend herself. Her father, Herbert, identified her.

Physical clues were still being sought. Much of the girls' clothing was missing and the river from Richmond to Erith in Kent was searched by the river police. Bicycle dealers were told to be on the look out for anyone selling them a new Phillips maroon-coloured sports cycle, K.29421. This was Barbara's bicycle. Lodging house keepers, hoteliers and cleaners were asked to watch for any bloodstained clothing. Appeals for any information about anyone who was missing from home on the night of 31 May and lived near Teddington were also issued.

The inquests on both victims were held at Kingston on 9 June. Dr Mant, a Home Office pathologist, detailed the medical evidence. In the case of Barbara, these were a fractured skull, a stab wound to the forehead and three to the chest. She had been sexually assaulted. Christine's injuries were similar, but rather more numerous; with ten stab wounds to the chest and two skull fractures. She had likewise been assaulted. Mant stated, 'Both the deceased were virgo intact before the assaults took place and in both cases the injuries were inflicted with great violence and were of similar nature and appeared to be inflicted with the same weapon. In both cases the sexual assault was of the most violent type.' The type of weapon used was a double-edged knife of about seven inches in length. The coroner then concluded:

> These are appalling crimes, and it may well be that there is some member of the public who could, even at this stage, assist the police with their difficult enquiries by coming forward with some information even if it appears to that member of the public to be information possibly of a trivial or insignificant nature. The police are obviously faced with a difficult and protracted inquiry.

Unfortunately, the next few weeks were inconclusive, despite a number of leads emerging. The disused Ham dock was dragged. Likewise, gravel pits near Teddington Lock were dragged. Nothing significant was found in any of these places. Grass near to the Thames was mowed in order to find clues, especially the weapon used. An anonymous letter from a Miss AG, who claimed she knew both girls, was received. A bloodstained towel was located in a train in Bournemouth, but its provenance was discovered and dismissed. Suspicious men were reported. One was a man seen on a woman's bicycle on the towpath on 31 May. Another was a man seen that night with a gleaming object in his hand, walking down Fairfax Road in Teddington at 11pm. He was aged between thirty-thirty-five, of medium build, wore glasses and was five feet eight or nine inches in height.

Altogether, the police held a press conference twice a day. They interviewed 7,000 people and called at 4,000 houses. A total of 1,657 written statements were taken, 4,987 questionnaires returned and 2,052 telephone messages were taken. This was a major investigation and it made national news.

It was noted that the murders had occurred on the night of a full moon. On 27 June, there was another full moon. Some thought that the killer might strike again or might revisit the scene of his crime. Some even thought that the murders were motivated by some kind of moon insanity. Police patrolled the towpath that night, but found nothing.

Although the police seemed to be making little progress, the killer struck again. On 12 June, Mrs Mary Birch was taking her dog for a walk in Windsor Great Park. A man asked her the way to Holly Tree. He then grabbed her mouth and throat and tried to pull her into the bushes. She briefly broke free and shouted for help. Then he attacked again. Although he did not rape or kill her – he was probably too frightened to do so – he took 17s from her before escaping.

Five days later, two policemen (PCs Howard and Oliver) were travelling in their patrol car along Oxshott Common. It was 5.40 pm. They were travelling to Kingston with two labourers, Bernard Hannam and Henry Bedford. Apparently, the latter had seen one Alfred Whiteway and contacted the police and they sent a patrol car there for him. On the Common they saw another man. He was taken into the car and sat in the back alone when the other two were dropped off, whilst the policemen sat in the front seats.

Alfred Charles Whiteway was a labourer who lived on Sydney Road, Teddington, and had been born on 21 June 1931. He had recently been employed for three months at the Decca Record Company. One of a family of eight, he was poorly educated, as was the rest of the family. Few had fond memories of him at this time, one Albert Newcombe, a school fellow, recalling, 'He regarded him as a bully.' The headmaster of Cotswold Approved School where he was sent in 1946 said he was 'foul mouthed, cruel to animals and lethargic'. Yet he was not a sociable man, he 'never had a mate and did not mix with other boys'. Since leaving Stanley Road Boys' Senior School in 1945 he had had a number of menial labouring jobs, including being an errand boy, a sprayer at a factory, a tree-feller, a builder's labourer and a lorry driver's mate; none of which lasted very long.

On 27 February 1952, he married Nellie Mary Jones (born 6 January 1935), who was pregnant (her mother would not give her permission to marry him otherwise) – she gave birth on 20 May 1952 and another child was due in August 1953. Mrs Jones retained her dislike for him, the police noting, 'Her mother with who she lives does not like her husband and will not allow him in her house.' Apparently he met his wife to be in May 1951 when he followed two young women along a street late one night – the other girl (Miss Isaac) later thought she had seen a knife in his hand, but his wife claimed this was not the case.

Whiteway already had a criminal record. He had five previous convictions for theft. On 21 April 1952, he had been sentenced to six months for stealing clothing and jewellery to the value of £20. Because he was in prison for most of the remainder of the year, he was unable to commit any more assaults.

Although strong, he had a poor heart so was not accepted for National Service. Not everyone had bad words for

Whiteway. His wife, who was not very bright, said of him, 'He has always been perfectly decent to me and our sex life was perfectly normal.' His sister said, 'He was always good tempered in the house, used to lark about and sing.' She added that he had only hit her the once. Harry Bedford, who had briefly been Whiteway's employer in 1952, said of him, that he was 'quiet and inoffensive', but a fellow worker, Bernard Hannam remarked that 'he did not think he was all there'. He was seen as a good worker, but a bad time keeper. He was briefly detained at Kingston police station, before being allowed to leave.

On 29 June, he was asked to account for his movements in the early hours of 1 June. Clearly he was a suspect for the double murder. He was ready with an answer, stating, 'I can tell you where I was, because I visited my wife.' Whiteway lived apart from his wife (who lived in King's Road), not because of any ill feeling between them, but because of the housing shortage, and resided with his widowed mother. He met his wife that night, but did not travel anywhere near the towpath and came home via Kingston Bridge and Sandy Lane at 11.55 pm. He was cycling. He added that he had been acquainted with the Songhurst family, having lived near her family, 'I knew Barbara when she was about six, but I have not seen her since. I did not know Christine Reed.'

Police enquiries into Whiteway continued. On 1 July, Hannam questioned him because he had been seen with a bicycle similar to one seen by Kathleen. He confessed to attacking her, adding, 'I don't know what made me do it.' Whiteway was then asked about the Teddington murders, and he told him, 'Guessed this would come before long. It looks like me, I grant you, but I will save you a lot of time by telling you that when that job was done I was with my wife at home.' He was further evasive when pressed about whether he knew where the girls were murdered, when he answered, 'I am going to keep my mouth shut, or you will pin this one on me. I had nothing to do with the girls. I would not go that far. You are wasting your time. The bloke who did that job was mad.' Hannam then had Whiteway's house searched for the axe he believed was used in the crime. It was not found.

On the next day, Whiteway was charged with the attack on Mrs Birch. He confessed to the deed, saying, 'I am the person who attacked the woman. I want to get it squared up.'

This added fuel to the police's case against him. Hannam thought he was on the track and kept questioning Whiteway. On 8 July, he made a significant and lengthy statement, which was taken down in writing. It was then that Whiteway's fascination with knives became apparent. He said, 'I have always been very fond of knives. I have only one at the present time, a sheath knife. Sometimes I carry one or more knives in the saddle-bag of my bicycle. That is when I go out for a bit of practice throwing. The last time I had knives in the saddle-bag was about eight weeks ago.' He further told how he had once been near the Teddington Lock, and, meeting a stranger, had a knife throwing contest, though they lost the two knives, one being a sheath knife, the other being a Gurkha knife. He also liked axes, stating, 'I can also throw a chopper at trees, in fact I throw it better than I do knives. Sometimes I take my mother's chopper in my saddle-bag when I go throwing.' When asked where the chopper was, he said that the police at Kingston had it, 'I put it in the police car under the seat. When they picked me up I had it tucked in my shirt... I pushed it under the seat with my foot.'

Next day, Whiteway was charged with assaulting Kathleen Ringham. This was even more damning because part of it directly impinged on the double murder at Teddington. Again, he confessed, saying, 'I made up my mind to seduce her and had got the chopper out of my saddle-bag. I caught up with her on the footpath, and I hit her on the head with the blunt end of the chopper.'

On 15 July, PC Arthur Cosh, a patrol car driver, had an embarrassing revelation to make. On 18 June, the day after Whiteway's ride in the patrol car, Cosh had found an axe in the back of the same car, hidden under the driver's seat, with the handle protruding. He took the axe and put it in his locker in the police garage. He went on sick leave on 23 June, returning to work on 8 July. He then took the axe home and put it in his tool box. He later used it to chop up sticks. He did not examine it and on 15 July he talked to PC Oliver about the matter. It was then that Cosh handed the axe over to Hannam. The axe was later identified by Miss Ivy Whiteway, Whiteway's sister.

On the same day, Whiteway was asked to account for his movements on the night of 31 May. That afternoon he had had an argument with his wife, then returned home, but at 7.45 pm, cycled around Richmond Park. At about 10 pm he went to see his wife at a shed in Canbury Gardens. They made up and then went to her home and had a cup of tea on her doorstep. He said that he left his wife between 11.30–11.35 pm. He then cycled home via Bentall's clock, Sandy Lane and Broad Street (a longer route than taking the towpath, but an easier ride), arriving home at five to midnight. He did not cycle anywhere near the towpath, so he said.

Whiteway was questioned again by Hannam on 30 July and was confronted with the physical evidence against him. He was shown the axe, and commented, 'Blimey, that's it. It's been – about. It was sharp when I had it. I sharpened it.' The Gurkha knife which he had mentioned had also been found and Whiteway remarked, 'That's it. You got it out of the water, didn't you?' Another piece of evidence was the fact that bloodstains had been found on Whiteway's right shoe. Whiteway denied this, stating, 'I don't believe it. I think you are putting one over me.' He later added, 'Were you kidding about blood on my shoe?' Hannam assured him he was being deadly serious. Hannam then saw Whiteway tremble and reply, 'You know well it was me, don't you? I didn't mean to kill 'em. I never wanted to hurt anyone.'

He also made the following statement:

> It's all up. You know well I done it, eh? That shoe's me. What a mess. I'm mental. Me head must be wrong. I must have a woman. I cannot stop myself. I'm not a murderer. B- them, yes, every time, but not kill 'em. I only saw one girl, she came around a tree where I stood and I bashed her and she was down like a log. The other screamed out down by the lock. Never saw her till then I didn't. I nipped over and shut her up. Two of 'em and then I tumbled the other one knew me. If it hadn't been for that it wouldn't have happened. Put that chopper away, it haunts yer. What more do they want to

> know. I b- them both, that is what I cannot stop. Why don't the doctors do something. It will be mental, won't it? It must be. I cannot stop it. Once you tell you a lie. Give us it. I will sign it.

A statement was written and signed, and Hannam told him that Barbara's bicycle and the knife used to commit the murders were still missing. Whiteway ignored the comment and told him, 'You have done it on me. I shall say its all lies, like the blood. You can tear that last one up. I didn't do it.'

When Hannam next spoke to Whiteway, the latter had a solicitor with him. Whiteway was charged with the double murder, which he denied.

On 15 September, Whiteway appeared before Richmond magistrates, in order to determine whether there was enough evidence for him to be put on trial at the Old Bailey. The facts of the case and the examinations of Whiteway by the police, which have already been stated, were gone through by Mr J F Claxton, prosecuting. Mr A C Prothero, defending, announced, 'My instructions are that the defendant emphatically denies the conversation which Mr Claxton told you about.' Prothero suggested that the statements allegedly made by Whiteway were highly dubious and should not be admitted as unbiased evidence. Yet the magistrates concluded on 18 September that the case should be heard before the Old Bailey.

The trial began on 27 October. The forensic evidence was discussed; although there were human bloodstains on Whiteway's right shoe, as if attempts had been made to wash the rest off, there was no blood on the axe that was his. The knife and the axe from the lads' camp had also been checked but nothing untoward was found on these, either. The next witness was Kathleen Ringham, who was about to recount her experience with Whiteway on Oxshott Heath, but she was interrupted by the defending counsel, and not allowed to finish her testimony – after all, the case was about the double murder, not her assault. The prosecution also relied heavily on the statements that Whiteway made to the police, but the defence said that these could not be taken as proof of anything.

The defence said that their task was not to show who the killer was, but to show that it was not Whiteway. They claimed that the bloodstain on the shoe occurred when he had an accident at work, and that he was nowhere near the towpath when the murders occurred. Whiteway admitted that he had once worked with Daniel Songhurst, Barbara's brother, and did know her slightly, as they lived in the same road as he did, eight years previously. He said that the statements he had signed were not true and that he did not kill the two girls. Although his wife and mother-in-law testified to his being with them on that night, they admitted that they might have got the times wrong. The trial concluded on 2 November. However after forty-five minutes of discussion, the jury decided that Whiteway was guilty and so he was sentenced to death.

Whiteway wrote to Hannam from his condemned cell on 12 November, taking the same line as his defence had. Part of the letter ran thus:

> Mr Hannam, you were wrong. Why you made up that false confession I can't say but you know that your word would be more accepted than mine.

An appeal was heard on 7 December. This was on the grounds that the jury were aware of Whiteway's previous record and this may have swayed their judgement. The police evidence was alleged again to have been concocted and the defendant's alibi was stressed. However, the appeal was dismissed and, on Tuesday 22 December 1953, Whiteway was hanged at Wandsworth prison.

What actually happened on the towpath is difficult to ascertain. It was clearly a brief scene of terror and bloody horror, as Whiteway attacked one girl and then the other, perhaps stunning them with the back of the axe, before assaulting them. Perhaps he then used the knife because he recognised Barbara and feared she might identify him. Therefore, both had to be silenced and he proceeded to murder them with a great deal of violence. He then tossed the bodies and bicycles into the Thames, cleaned himself and his weapons up as best he could, and cycled home. Whiteway was motivated by lust for violent sex and the only consolation must be that he was speedily caught, tried and hanged.

Conclusion

s well as being a pleasant place to live and an enjoyable place for a day out, the Thameside villages which now form the boroughs of Richmond and Kingston have also been the scenes of suicide and murder. Some of these made national headlines.

Of the murders recounted here, most of the victims were female and most of the killers were men, as is usually the case. To be exact, of these crimes, ten women, seven men and three children were killed. Their killers were fourteen men and two women. In most cases, the killer and victim were already been acquainted, often being family members or living in the same household, except in chapters 8 and 17. Two of the killers here claimed two victims and one killed three. Their methods varied, with seven being killed by gunshot wounds, six dying from bladed instruments; three were bludgeoned and four strangled. The motives of the killers were also diverse. Employment disputes, sex, insanity and unknown motives all accounted for three murders each, with rage resulting in one death and burglary another. In only two crimes was money the reason for murder. The criminals met different fates. Four committed suicide, four were hanged, four were gaoled and four escaped justice.

In most cases the reader will pity the victims. Some of the killers, though, may evoke sympathy from the reader, Maurice Odell Tribe being one. Others, though, merit none, and perhaps Whiteway was the most vicious. Some of the cases recounted are puzzles. Did Dr Smethurst kill his wife? Probably not. Did Hadfield kill Mrs Mordaunt-Chapman? Probably. But who killed James Wells and why?

In many cases, the amount of detection required by the police was minimal. Some killers simply gave themselves up, such as Jack Martin and William Baldwin, and in others, detection was assisted by the criminal committing similar crimes, such as Whiteway. The police were often painstaking in their enquiries, but in no cases was there a brilliant detective. Some cases were probably unsolvable once the crime had been committed and the culprit fled the scene – the murder of PC Atkins being one of these.

In most cases, modern comparisons with crimes of years gone by are unfavourable. Yet Richmond and Kingston prove the exceptions. Police figures for April 2007-March 2009 indicate that there have been no murders at all in these districts; whereas the average for these places from the 1930s–1950s is one per year (still a relatively low number). Elsewhere in London, the figures are less impressive – there have been thirty-four murders in Lambeth from 2007–09. If current trends continue, the inhabitants of Richmond and Kingston are doubly favoured.

Appendix

Other murders committed in Richmond and Kingston, 1891–1957.

17 August 1891:	Frances Beresford killed her mother, Georgina, at Twickenham.
1 December 1898:	Mary Dick strangled her daughter, Dorothy, in Kingston.
12 March 1899:	Herbert Goodall killed his wife and two children, in Twickenham.
8 March 1902:	Charles Earl killed Mary Pamphilon, at Mortlake.
9 November 1902:	Rebecca Brown was killed by William Brown, in Mortlake.
4 May 1904:	Alfred Hedley was shot by his father, Reginald, in Richmond.
11 September 1906:	Alma Auspach was shot by his cousin, Carl Reynol, in Richmond.
20 September 1913:	Edith Court was killed by Wolfram Court, in Kingston.
25 September 1914:	Jane Weston was killed by her husband, Henry, in Richmond.
17 December 1915:	Ada Elms drowned her children, in Twickenham.
19 September 1915:	Sarah Poynter gassed Patricia and Doris Clearly, in Richmond.
24 May 1923:	Ada Kerr was killed by Henry Griffon, in Whitton.
22 May 1933:	Annie Bennett was killed by her father, William, in Ashford.
6 November 1934:	Louisa Harris was killed on the Barnes towpath, by George Newman.
20 August 1935:	Leonard Day killed his wife and three children, in Tolworth.
3 March 1937:	Douglas Scott killed Sarah Scott, in Worcester Park.

30 May 1937:	An unknown baby was found dead in Twickenham.
2 September 1937:	Gertrude Hogg was killed by Ada Walsh in Kingston.
26 May 1938:	Peter Rampton was killed near Barnes Station, by Mr Eastwood.
5 January 1941:	Annie Jopling was killed by Eva Jopling, in Mortlake.
7 January 1942:	Lillian Stuart was killed by Gladys, her mother, in Surbiton.
26 December 1943:	Joan Thompson was killed by Lucy, her mother, in Barnes.
2 July 1944:	Ernest Dawkins was killed by Mabel Minnion, at Surbiton.
17 November 1945:	Daphne Hartley was shot by Emmanuel Carday, at Barnes Common.
20 January 1946:	Ann Woolley was killed by Winifred Woolley, at Worcester Park.
26 March 1948:	William Silver was killed by Norris Megaw, at Teddington.
26 September 1953:	John Conroy was killed by Teresa Conroy, at Twickenham.
8 March 1954:	Patrick Webb was killed by Harriett Webb, at Surbiton.
9 May 1954:	Nellie Officer was strangled by Rupert Wells, at Kingston.
3 March 1955:	A baby was found dead in Twickenham.
2 May 1957:	Annie Waters was killed by Thomas Bennett, at Kingston.

Information from The National Archives, Police Murder and Manslaughter files, MEP020/1-5

NB: Method of recording murders from 1918-31 may mean the number of murders at this time not recorded here.

Bibliography

Primary sources

(1) Manuscript
The National Archives:
CRIM 1/99/9 (Seddon); 1/583 (Seddon); 1/1103 (Desnos); MEPO3/107 (Martin); 129 (Earley); 1588 (Whitton); 1626 (Filson); 1632 (Oliver); 1665 (Isaacson); 1712 (Mordaunt-Chapman); 1724 (Dancy); 1737 (Key), 3001 (Martin); 9537 (Songhurst and Reed); 4/2 (police deaths); 20/1-5 (registers of murders, 1891-1958). WO339/ 29061, Maurice Odell Tribe

Principal Division of the Family
Indexes to Wills

London Metropolitan Archives
MS8241/6 and 8239/5 (Society of Apothecaries)
MS 11936/541 Sun Insurance Company
St Mark's Kennington Bishop's transcripts

Surrey History Centre
ES12/25/Bradish1

(2) Printed
Army Lists
Baedeaker's London and its Environs, (1900)
M S Briggs, *Middlesex Old and New* (1934)
*Dickens' The Thames Guide (*1887)
The Gentleman's Magazine, 1812
Kingston directories
Medical directories, 1848-1977
The Medical Times and Gazette, 1859
The Richmond and Twickenham Times, 1877, 1879, 1894, 1905, 1927, 1936, 1937, 1953
Richmond directories
The Surrey Comet, 1861, 1881, 1888, 1938, 1939, 1948

J Thorne, *Environs of London* (1876)
The Times, 1812, 1859, 1872, 1879, 1881, 1888, 1894, 1936, 1953
The West London Observer, 1894, 1937
Kingston and Richmond electoral registers

Electronic resources
Ancestry.com
Oldbaileyonline
The Times online
1841–1911 Census

Secondary Sources
R Altick, *Victorian Studies in Scarlet* (1970)
J Cloake, *Richmond Past* (1991)
Dixon, *Corridors of Times* (1903)
A Duncan, 'Bloodshed in Barnes', *The Wick* (June, 1995)
M Fido, *Murder Guide to London* (1988)
J H Lodge, *Famous Trials* (1961)
L A Parry, *Some Famous Medical Trials* (1927)
F Barker and D Silvester-Carr, *Black Plaque Guide to London* (1987)

Index